Editor-in-Chief and Founder:
Lyndon H. LaRouche, Jr.
Editorial Board: *Lyndon H. LaRouche, Jr. , Helga Zepp-LaRouche, Robert Ingraham, Tony Papert, Gerald Rose, Dennis Small, Jeffrey Steinberg, William Wertz*
Co-Editors: *Robert Ingraham, Tony Papert*
Managing Editor: *Nancy Spannaus*
Technology: *Marsha Freeman*
Books: *Katherine Notley*
Ebooks: *Richard Burden*
Graphics: *Alan Yue*
Photos: *Stuart Lewis*
Circulation Manager: *Stanley Ezrol*

INTELLIGENCE DIRECTORS
Counterintelligence: *Jeffrey Steinberg, Michele Steinberg*
Economics: *John Hoefle, Marcia Merry Baker, Paul Gallagher*
History: *Anton Chaitkin*
Ibero-America: *Dennis Small*
Russia and Eastern Europe: *Rachel Douglas*
United States: *Debra Freeman*

INTERNATIONAL BUREAUS
Bogotá: *Miriam Redondo*
Berlin: *Rainer Apel*
Copenhagen: *Tom Gillesberg*
Houston: *Harley Schlanger*
Lima: *Sara Madueño*
Melbourne: *Robert Barwick*
Mexico City: *Gerardo Castilleja Chávez*
New Delhi: *Ramtanu Maitra*
Paris: *Christine Bierre*
Stockholm: *Ulf Sandmark*
United Nations, N.Y.C.: *Leni Rubinstein*
Washington, D.C.: *William Jones*
Wiesbaden: *Göran Haglund*

ON THE WEB
e-mail: eirns@larouchepub.com
www.larouchepub.com
www.executiveintelligencereview.com
www.larouchepub.com/eiw
Webmaster: *John Sigerson*
Assistant Webmaster: *George Hollis*
Editor, Arabic-language edition: *Hussein Askary*

EIR (ISSN 0273-6314) *is published weekly (50 issues), by EIR News Service, Inc., P.O. Box 17390, Washington, D.C. 20041-0390. (703) 777-9451*

European Headquarters: E.I.R. GmbH, Postfach Bahnstrasse 9a, D-65205, Wiesbaden, Germany Tel: 49-611-73650
Homepage: http://www.eirna.com
e-mail: eirna@eirna.com
Director: Georg Neudecker

Montreal, Canada: 514-461-1557

Denmark: EIR - Danmark, Sankt Knuds Vej 11, basement left, DK-1903 Frederiksberg, Denmark. Tel.: +45 35 43 60 40, Fax: +45 35 43 87 57. e-mail: eirdk@hotmail.com.

Mexico City: EIR, Sor Juana Inés de la Cruz 242-2 Col. Agricultura C.P. 11360
Delegación M. Hidalgo, México D.F.
Tel. (5525) 5318-2301
eirmexico@gmail.com

Canada Post Publication Sales Agreement #40683579

Postmaster: Send all address changes to *EIR*, P.O. Box 17390, Washington, D.C. 20041-0390.

Signed articles in *EIR* represent the views of the authors, and not necessarily those of the Editorial Board.

On the Edge of War

EDITORIAL

You Have the Keys To Stop the Terror Wave: Use Them!

June 13—The mass murder rampage in Orlando, Florida, by alleged Islamic State follower Omar Mateen, is but the latest in a series of horrific terrorist attacks that all flow from a thirty-year-old "oil deal" between the British and Saudi monarchies. That deal has given them great power and great hidden resources to create today's global jihadist apparatus, for attacks against nations.

Until and unless that Anglo-Saudi apparatus is exposed—as we can do with the exposure of the 9/11 documents kept secret for 15 years—and dismantled, the world will face blind terrorist attacks constantly, in any locale at any time.

President Obama became a knowing and willing agent of the British and Saudis in his perpetual wars, which have spread chaos across the Mideast and North Africa, and terrorism across the world.

What a "coincidence" that Obama is meeting today with Saudi Crown Prince Salman in Washington, while his CIA Director, John Brennan, is going all out to try to "exonerate" Saudi Arabia from its role in setting up the 9/11 attacks and killing 3,000 Americans. Both Obama and Prince Salman meet with bloody hands.

EIR Founding Editor Lyndon LaRouche noted, today, that he has been aware of this British/Saudi power for evil for decades; and that this contributed to his making a very public, published warning back on Jan. 3, 2001, that a major terrorist attack on the United States was threatened in the Fall of 2001.

"We are still dealing with the same case, even in yesterday's mass murder in Orlando," LaRouche said.

The young Orlando killer had gone to Saudi Arabia in 2011 and in 2012, while employed by the British international security firm G4S; and came back an apparently very changed personality.

LaRouche emphasized that because Obama's wars are leading immediately now into a confrontation with Russia, and threatening World War III, it is essential to expose the Saudi/British hands—starting with 9/11— and force Obama out.

The 'Deal' that Launched 1,000 Attacks

In 1985, Prince Bandar bin-Sultan, the Saudi Ambassador to the United States, entered into a long-term partnership with the British government of then-Prime Minister Margaret Thatcher. Under the cover of an oil-for-weapons agreement called Al-Yamamah (Arabic for "the dove"), the British and Saudi monarchies established an offshore fund which grew to huge proportions, and has been used for conducting global terrorism against targeted nations.

During the more than 30 years since Al-Yamamah was launched, the British and Saudi monarchies have amassed well over $100 billion in a string of offshore secret funds, o finance terrorism, assassinations, coup plots and other crimes like the current Saudi/British/ U.S. invasion and bombing of Yemen.

Under Al-Yamamah, the British arms manufacturer BAE Systems provided an estimated $40 billion in weapons to the Saudi Ministry of Defense and Aviation, and an additional estimated $20 billion in bribes to Saudi princes and defense officials. In return, the Saudis provided 600,000 barrels of oil per day to the British. Through the Anglo-Dutch oil giants British Petroleum and Royal Dutch Shell, the oil was sold on the international spot markets, generating hundreds of billions of dollars in profits. An *EIR* study in 2007 estimated that at minimum, $100 billion in excess funds was amassed and deposited in offshore secret bank accounts for use in joint Anglo-Saudi covert operations.

In an official biography, Prince Bandar boasted of using these covert funds, and of the special nature of the Al-Yamamah deal, which could have only been carried out between two monarchies that could act above the law and blur the distinctions between public and private actions.

ISIS, in other words, has definitely *not* been the world's richest Islamist terrorist operation.

In 2007, when British media conducted a limited expose of the Al-Yamamah bribery scandal, Prime

Minister Tony Blair shut down the investigation by Britain's Serious Fraud Office (SFO), on the grounds that the Anglo-Saudi partnership was essential to British national security. The shut-down order came within hours of a decision by the Swiss government to allow the SFO access to the secret bank accounts of Wafiq Said, a front man for the Al-Yamamah funds.

The Al-Yamamah deal was a lucrative transaction for Prince Bandar, who received a commission for his role in launching the program of at least $2 billion (U.S. intelligence sources estimate that Bandar received in excess of $10 billion on the deal).

In the Matter of 3,000 Americans Killed

Bandar is directly implicated in the Sept. 11, 2001, attacks on the World Trade Center and the Pentagon. Funds from the personal bank account of Bandar and his wife Princess Haifa (sister of Saudi intelligence's longtime director Prince Turki al-Faisal) were passed to two of the original 9/11 hijackers, Khalid al-Mihdhar and Nawaf al-Hazmi, through Saudi intelligence officers Omar al-Bayoumi and Osama Basnan. Funds went from the Bank of England accounts of the British Ministry of Defence's Defense Export Support Office (DESO) to Bandar's account at Riggs National Bank. In addition, al-Bayoumi and Basnan received funding through a ghost employment with a Saudi defense firm, Dalah Aviation, which was a sole contractor for the Saudi Defense Ministry.

A Federal Judge in Sarasota, Fla., is now reviewing more than 80,000 pages of suppressed FBI documents dealing with a Sarasota cell of the 9/11 hijackers and its links to a prominent Saudi wealthy businessman with strong ties to the Saudi Monarchy. Weeks before the 9/11 attacks, the Saudi family residing in a gated community in Sarasota abruptly left the country. They left possessions behind indicating that they were leaving on very short notice. The FBI conducted a lengthy investigation into the family, because they had hosted three of the 9/11 hijackers, including ring-leader Mohammed Atta on many occasions, according to security logs and video camera footage, showing Atta and the others entering and leaving the compound.

The FBI concealed the documents and the fact of the investigation from the Joint Inquiry and the 9/11 Commission. Former Sen. Bob Graham, who co-chaired the Joint Inquiry, now insists that the existence of the Saudi Royals' links to the Sarasota cell, when added to the evidence of the Saudi government support

for the San Diego cell, raises further questions about the 9/11 attack. What about Herndon, Virginia, and Paterson, New Jersey, Sen. Graham has publicly asked?

A 47-page document prepared by the two 9/11 Commission staffers who had earlier worked for the Joint Inquiry and had written the 28-page suppressed chapter, identified a total of 20 Saudi officials with proven ties to the 19 hijackers prior to the Sept. 11, 2001 attacks.

Those links went from southern California to the Saudi Embassy in Washington to the Saudi Embassy in Berlin, Germany. Former Secretary of the Navy John Lehman, a member of the 9/11 Commission, told *60 Minutes* that the Commission did not conduct an exhaustive investigation into the leads that should have been pursued related to the Saudi Monarchy and Saudi regime support for the hijackers. Lehman, among other commissioners, has called for a top-to-bottom new investigation into 9/11—one in which all of the suppressed leads and open trails to the Saudi Royals are pursued fully.

Over the thirty-plus years of the Al-Yamamah program, funds have gone through these offshore secret accounts, as well as through Saudi charities, to finance a global network of mosques and madrasas that have recruited generations to the extreme Wahhabi/Salafist apparatus that is the recruiting pool for Sunni jihadi terrorism worldwide.

What To Do

The evidence contained in the still-classified 28-page chapter from the original Joint Congressional Inquiry into 9/11, opens the door to unraveling the entire Anglo-Saudi terror operation. Without an understanding of the role of the British Monarchy and the British intelligence services in the jihad apparatus, it is impossible to shut down the capabilities.

The CIA Director insisted in an interview on Sunday that Americans "should not believe" that 28-page chapter, which he fears is about to be forced out, declassified. But one Republican member of Congress retorted in a tweet, "The CIA Director must be referring to a different 28 pages than the ones I read. Release them and let the American people decide."

You have the means in your hands to counterattack this British/Saudi operation. Use them. Force the Saudi evidence out. Force Obama out. "This must be done quickly," LaRouche said today, "to prevent further destruction internationally."

Peace Is Possible Only with Russia and China!

by Helga Zepp-LaRouche

June 11—"Nomen est omen"—the name is an omen— can be said of the NATO *Anakonda 16* maneuvers currently taking place in Poland with 31,000 soldiers involved. For while the exercise is supposed to defend against the supposed invasion of Poland and the Baltic States by an "adversary" (Russia, naturally), the name of the exercise—a snake that strangles its meals—betrays the actual intention of NATO, which has now advanced along the entire Eastern European border of Russia. Three other simultaneous maneuvers are being held in the Baltic states and Poland, so that 50-60,000 soldiers in all, are operating right on the border of Russia.

The last time this happened, it was the invasion of Hitler's Reichswehr in 1941—and that is exactly how the Russian population experiences it. The difference is that what is at stake this time is World War III and the use of thermonuclear weapons, and thus the end of mankind.

In parallel with *Anakonda 16*, three other maneuvers are underway—*Baltops 16* in and around the Baltic Sea, *Saber Strike 16* in the three Baltic republics, and *Swift Response 16* in Poland and Germany. There are no published figures on the exact size of these forces, but it can be estimated that between

Rear Admiral Bret Batchelder provocatively characterized the arrival of four U.S. Aegis Class destroyers and two U.S. aircraft carriers in the Black Sea—at the same time as four NATO maneuvers totaling 50-60,000 troops were being conducted along Russia's western borders—as a "clear demonstration of capacities."

www.public.navy.mil

50,000 and 60,000 soldiers are taking part in the four maneuvers combined. At the same time, the *USS Porter*—one of the four Aegis Class destroyers stationed in Rota, Spain, and a part of the U.S. ballistic missile defense (BMD) system—arrived in the Black Sea en route to the Bulgarian port of Varna. Simultaneously, the aircraft carrier *USS Dwight Eisenhower* entered the Mediterranean from the Atlantic, and the *USS Harry Truman* moved from the Persian Gulf through the Suez Canal to the U.S. European Command in the Mediterranean, in a "clear demonstration of capacities," as Rear Admiral Bret Batchelder put it.

Russia is reacting to these demonstrations by adding personnel to the military bases in its northern military district, holding exercises in Crimea and in the Rostov region and, according to *Izvestia*, conducting exercises in which Russian pilots practice neutralizing the American BMD installations along the Russian border.

What is the real purpose of this BMD system?

As Russian Deputy Defense Minister Anatoly Antonov recently emphasized at the Shangri-La Dialogue security conference in Singapore, Russia fears that the purpose of the U.S. BMD system being installed along the Russian border is to conduct a surprise strike on the Russian nuclear arsenal and incapacitate the defensive second strike. The pretext, transparent from the beginning, that this system is necessary to protect Europe from missile strikes from Iran, was vitiated no later than the P5+1 Agreement with Iran; and military experts agree that this system can be converted in an extremely short time from a defensive to an offensive missile system, simply by changing the software, without the host countries like Romania or Poland even noticing.

It has now dawned on some observers that this combination—the encirclement of Russia, maneuvers expressing an aggressive intention even in their name, and the expected counter-measures by Russia—has created a situation in which the critical moment of decision could be only minutes away. *Der Spiegel* worries that these maneuvers, based on a scenario of an actual war, are going too far. *Die Zeit* calls the installation of the BMD systems in Romania and Poland probably the greatest error NATO has ever committed, possibly leading to Russia canceling the Intermediate-Range Nuclear Forces (INF) Treaty.

One high-ranking military figure commented that these provocations against Putin are extremely foolish, because they can only lead to escalation. This situation very much recalls that prior to World War I, he said. If one side is confronted with the threat of losing face, that marks the start of war.

Of even greater concern is President Obama's refusal to even acknowledge, let alone discuss, Russia's security concerns over the U.S. BMD system, although President Putin has repeatedly requested such opportunities—most recently on May 27 of this year. Moscow has of course not failed to notice that NATO doctrine has long

commons.wikimedia.org

Russian Deputy Defense Minister Anatoly Antonov said that Russia knows that the U.S. missile system being installed along its border can rapidly be changed to an offensive system.

since departed from the doctrine of Mutually Assured Destruction (MAD) and has abandoned its premise, that using nuclear weapons is out of the question because it would lead to mutual and complete destruction. It has been replaced with the utopian doctrine that a limited nuclear attack is "winnable" because, thanks to modern technologies, the second-strike capacity of any adversary can be knocked out by means of a surprise attack. This idea was put forward[1] in 2006 in *Foreign Affairs*, the journal of the Council on Foreign Relations. Today it is the basis for various U.S. and NATO doctrines—that of Prompt Global Strike, of the U.S. BMD system, and of the Air-Sea Battle doctrine for Asia. That Obama refuses even to discuss the Russian issues and arguments, raised again by Anatoly Antonov, can only be interpreted in one way, in the eyes of many observers.

_____

1. See https://www.foreignaffairs.com/articles/united-states/2006-03-01/rise-us-nuclear-primacy

en.wikipedia.org

Here President Putin (left) meets President Obama in New York, Sept. 29, 2015. Russian Deputy Defense Minister Antonov noted that Obama refuses to discuss Russia's concerns about the provocative actions being taken against it.

Russian Consul General Sergey Petrov stated at a June 8 Schiller Institute conference in San Francisco that "we are very close to a major conflict," and added that if a "limited nuclear war" is started, "it will be the end of the world."

That conclusion is supported by the bellicose tone adopted by the "new guard" of American military commanders. Thus Lt. General Ben Hodges, Commander of U.S. Forces Europe, stressed that NATO's position in the Baltic states has shifted from assurance to "deterrence." "Deterrence" requires the actual presence of military capacities that render the adversary incapable of attaining his objectives; it does not involve a tripwire, which only triggers the intervention of the full strategic arsenal. "We need Russia in the international community," said Hodges, "but it only respects strength."

Russia has repeatedly stressed that it does not have the slightest intention of invading the Baltic states or Poland—yet this scenario is the basis for the entire hysteria. Early this year the RAND Corporation published a study purporting to show that the Baltic states, due to a lack of strategic depth, could not be defended against

a Russian intervention, and could be overrun by Russian troops within 60 hours. The study thereby implicitly acknowledged that all the battalions and heavy equipment being transferred there will still perform only the function of a tripwire. Precisely this—according to Michael Carpenter, U.S. Deputy Secretary of Defense for Russia, Ukraine, and Eurasia, in testimony before the Senate Foreign Relations Committee—makes it necessary to quadruple the Pentagon's spending for Europe in 2017.

Europe as Cannon Fodder?

It is literally one minute to midnight. Survival demands that we wake up, before we in Europe are sacrificed as cannon fodder in a supposedly limited nuclear war to the geopolitical interests of the Anglo-American empire, an empire whose claim to rule over a unipolar world can no longer be sustained. If, at the NATO summit in Warsaw in early July, there is a further buildup of the U.S. BMD system—planned, among other things, is the linking of the system in Romania with the missile-capable Aegis destroyers—then the point of no return could be reached very soon.

At the most recent conference of the Schiller Institute, the Russian Consul-General in San Francisco answered a question on this subject from former U.S. Senator Mike Gravel, and made the point. "I share the understanding that we are very close to a major conflict. And I add that there is no possibility of a 'limited nuclear war.' If that starts, it will be end of the world."

It is high time to leave NATO and replace it with an inclusive security architecture that allows all of us to survive. Federal Chancellor Merkel's walking on eggs—striving for an EU-Russia common economic space "in the long run," but approving the extension of the EU sanctions against Russia for another six months—is immensely dangerous. The "Christian" Democratic Union politician should know what the Bible had to say, in *Revelation* 3:15, about being lukewarm.

EIR Contents

www.larouchepub.com Volume 43, Number 25, June 17, 2016

Cover This Week

These paratroopers on this year's NATO maneuvers are part of the largest military mobilization on Russia's western border since World War II.

I. The Manhattan Project

THE BATTLE FOR AMERICA IN MANHATTAN!

'Murder, Though It Have No Tongue, Will Speak'

by Dennis Speed

What tends to cause many people to defeat themselves before the battle starts, in facing tyrants, is the widespread popular delusion, that the tyrant is either too powerful, or simply too popular, to be engaged. Popular opinion, in its habituated credulity in such matters, fails to grasp the fact, that, often, the tyrant is, at bottom, a stage figure.

> — Lyndon LaRouche, "George Bush and the 'Ibykus Principle,'" 1996

America is now at a moment when President Barack Obama is leading the world to the precipice of World War III. Military provocations against both Russia and China, including the largest deployment of hostile troops on the western border of Russia since the Nazi invasion of 1941, have dramatically escalated, even within just recent weeks, and the imminent danger to all of humanity is intense.

This same Obama also continues to back ISIS terrorists in Syria as part of his insane vendetta against Syrian President Assad, the very same ISIS terrorists who now claim responsibility for the massacre at the Orlando, Florida nightclub. Obama also continues to

There is a widespread popular delusion, that the tyrant is either too powerful, or simply too popular, to be engaged. Popular opinion, in its habituated credulity, fails to grasp that often, the tyrant is, at bottom, a stage figure.

refuse to release the 28 pages from the Congressional Joint Inquiry into 9/11, pages which prove Saudi sponsorship for the 2001 attack on American soil that claimed thousands of American lives.

Then there is the matter of Obama's infamous "kill sessions," held for months every Tuesday in the White House, where Obama, personally, picks the names of those individuals, including American citizens, to be assassinated through U.S. drone strikes. If innocents die, that is simply acceptable collateral damage. As Bush CIA and NSA chief Michael Hayden said about Obama's assassination of U.S. citizen Anwar al Awlaki, "We needed a court order to eavesdrop on him, but we [i.e., Obama] didn't need a court order to kill him. Isn't that something?"

Whether the Tuesday White House killing sessions still go on formally or not, everyone in the United States government knows that Obama is in the practice of regularly ordering the execution of various "enemies of the state"—on Tuesdays, and other days of the week. This includes Americans. Former Obama supporters have been more terrified because of this, than perhaps any other manifestation of the true Obama that is made known to them.

Obama is a murderer. He is also insane. The fact that he is not identified, or certified, as insane, does not change the truth of the nation's predicament. The Obama campaign to shut down the manned space flight program, as well as the space program as a whole, is the potential "point of no return" for the United States. Obama objected to a continuation of manned exploration of the Moon with the deranged assertion, "we've already done that."

Go Along To Get Along

American author and lawyer Glenn Greenwald, in his afterword to Jeremy Scahill's recently published book, *The Assassination Complex*, states:

Barack Obama's 2008 Presidential campaign is, for many, a distant memory. For that reason it is easy to forget that his vows to reverse the core strategy of the Bush-Cheney war on terror were central, not ancillary, to his electoral victory … It is hard to overstate the conflict between Obama's statements before he became president and his presidential actions.

Slightly later, however, Greenwald brings up the

LPAC

The LaRouche movement, here on the streets of New York City, is organizing for the urgent impeachment of President Obama to avoid World War III.

matter upon which our attention and reflection are immediately focussed: the unseemly adoption in recent decades by Americans of a slave mentality of "go along to get along," even of going along with murder and madness. ("One must be practical in these matters, you know.") Greenwald writes:

Obama did not navigate this transformation alone. As is to be expected in the highly partisan and polarized political climate that prevails in the United States, large numbers of Democrats and progressives transformed with him from virulent critics of these policies to vocal supporters once they became Obama policies rather than Bush policies.

If we accept what Greenwald writes to be true, we must conclude that much of the American 2008 electoral base either never had any morality at all to inform their purported "principled" choice for Obama as President, or they gave away, or were corrupted away, from whatever that morality was. The only difference between the earlier Bush and later Obama administrations, is that under Obama, the killing became more efficient, widespread, and routine than it had been earlier. The American people tolerate it, not because they agree with it, but because of *fear*—"nameless, unreasoning, unjustified terror, which paralyzes needed efforts to convert retreat into advance"—the condition against which Franklin Roosevelt warned the nation on March 4, 1933, in his First Inaugural Address.

Let's Play a Game Called 'Fear'

Fear itself is a powerful self-brainwashing force. British subject and Tavistock Institute brainwasher

R.D. Laing codified "the politics of fear" in the beginning of a short book he entitled *Knots*. It accurately describes the distilled thought process of the British subject's slave mentality:

> They are playing a game. They are playing at not playing a game. If I show them I see they are, I shall break the rules and they will punish me. I must play their game, of not seeing I see the game.

This is the essence of what is called "game theory," the game theory of people such as Bertrand Russell, who from no later than 1900 were working overtime to break the American revolutionary spirit that Alexander Hamilton exemplified in his, Franklin's, Washington's, and others' refusal to play the game of bowing to the mad King of England. Their Declaration of Independence was a non-negotiable fight for the sovereignty of the creativity of the human mind as the highest authority in the world—not the arbitrary "divine right" of not-so-divine Kings, Emperors, and Obamas, over life and death.

If you are trying to implement the American Presidency, the American Constitution, and the American economy designed and defended by Alexander Hamilton in the American Revolution, it doesn't much help to have the moral direct descendant of "Mad King George the Third" in the White House. There is no need to search for Barack Obama's birth certificate when you face the fact that, in his commitment to upholding British Crown interests, he is more directly a descendant of the Bush family than, for example, his hapless would-be sibling Jeb. "For Ernst Cassell begat E.H. Harriman, who begat Prescott Bush, who begat George Herbert Walker, who begat G.W. and begat Barack Obama."

At this point the credulous would begin to tremble with fear. Visions of Skull and Bones, Freemasonry, and various Satanic cults dance in their heads, and with good reason. When one says, "FBI," one has pronounced the name of Bush, the name of Wall Street, and the name of Her Satanic Majesty. But these forces only rule the night through fear, and Alexander Hamilton's Presidential system was designed to expose them to the

Public domain/Herman Hiller/Library of Congress

If you wish to end slavery, Malcolm X insisted, you must first end the slave mentality. Here, Malcolm X after his 1964 pilgrimage to Mecca.

light, and remove them from wielding power over the American people.

The Obama killing machine that, so far as anyone knows, still meets every Tuesday, *could be dismantled "on any Wednesday"* by American citizens who would join forces to act to remove Obama from power. True, impeachment and removal from office should have been visited upon the preceding Cheney-Bush Administration—but it was not. The notion that impeachment, or the removal of Obama, would now be adequately accomplished "through the normal electoral process" is also untrue. A comparison of Cheney/Bush's military policies with those of Obama, demonstrates why. Without removing Obama, no part of the human race knows for sure that it will even see tomorrow.

Manhattan: the Battleground

Organizers for Lyndon LaRouche's *Manhattan Project* in New York City have considerable contact every day with tens of thousands of Americans and non-Americans. They have face-to-face conversations with hundreds of people on street corners and in shopping districts. Organizers report that, once one gets below the surface response, the stark truth becomes evident—the American people are gripped precisely by that fear of which FDR spoke in 1933. The fear is not merely for their material situation—rent payments and the rest. The fear is that the nation is completely adrift, that its future mission is unclear or unknown, and that "I'm too small to do anything about it, because the current tyrant"—Obama—"is too powerful" or "too popular."

What might be the antidote to this sorry condition?

There is an old lesson, learned "the hard way," in the streets of 1960s America. It was taught in particular by Malcolm X to many, including the late Muhammad Ali. (Lyndon LaRouche personally witnessed Malcolm X teach this lesson to those that came to hear him in places like the Audubon Ballroom on Broadway and 165th Street in Harlem.) The principle was, "If you wish to end slavery, you must first end the slave mentality." And what is the typical expression of slave mentality? Harriet Tubman, who will shortly replace Andrew Jackson on the twenty dollar bill, put it this way: "I freed a thousand slaves. I could have freed a thousand more, *if they had known* they were slaves."

Tubman's expression, however, more precisely defines the mentality of the "British subject" than of the slave more generally. Obama is a puppet of the British Queen, and it is the mentality of a subject that he exudes, which is imitated by those either silly enough or terrified enough to pretend that he is much more than a "stage presence."

Some are intelligent enough to understand that in 2016 America, slavery is no longer "legally" confined, as it was in the Nineteenth Century, to African-Americans, but is, rather, the pervasive condition of the majority of American citizens—*as a current, British Empire-imposed, but reversible mental condition.* Most, however, refuse to admit that they are scared to death of Barack Obama, who murders people through an imperial prerogative called "special presidential powers" of the "unitary executive." These assassinations of Americans and non-Americans can be ordered regularly every Tuesday. People are afraid of Obama's predecessors, who were never punished for the crime of the illegal and unjust war of 2003 in Iraq, and they are afraid of— and even "pre-disgusted" by— whoever their successors are likely to be. That is why participation rates in American elections, particularly primaries, are inevitably dismally low.

S.H. Bradford, *Scenes in the Life of Harriet Tubman*

Harriet Tubman: "I freed a thousand slaves. I could have freed a thousand more, if they had known they were slaves." In this woodcut, Tubman is shown in her Civil War clothing.

Up from Slavery

There is a way to break through this contemporary "British subject/slave" mentality. Three examples illustrate what this way is.

Invited to participate in a Bronx Sunday Puerto Rican Day Parade, LaRouche associates made a banner which read, *"Dispierta y Lucha por La Humanidad"* (Stand Up and Fight for Humanity). It featured a large picture of the world's largest single-dish radio telescope, located in the city of Arecibo in Puerto Rico, and a picture of the famous cellist, Pablo Casals. Casals'

mother and wife were born in Puerto Rico. In 1957, he founded one of the world's great Classical music festivals there. There was no reference to the much-discussed "Puerto Rican debt crisis"—because there is no *Puerto Rican* debt crisis. The entire financial system is bankrupt, and only if people "look up, and stand up," can they win. This is the moral opposite of Obama, who does not believe the space program would, or should ever, solve the problems of the very poor people who mistakenly voted for him.

Recently, a LaRouche PAC squad deployed in an overwhelmingly African-American and Hispanic section of the Bronx. Its report included an account of a confrontation with a man who was so incensed at a sign depicting Obama behind bars—captioned, "Jail Obama For 9/11 Coverup"—that he wanted to overturn the organizers' table,— but changed his mind:

We were on Tremont Avenue in the South Bronx (the neighborhood made famous by Tom Wolfe's novel *Bonfire of the Vanities*) at the Post Office. People saw the sign as they walked toward us. Several people were asking why we would say such a thing about Obama. This was largely asked as a curious, not hostile question, though several people were inclined to support Obama. When the censoring of the [Congressional Joint Inquiry's] 28 pages on 9/11 was gone thorough, starting with the Bush Administration, and that Obama had continued the same practice, especially in not releasing the pages, and was still using 9/11 to justify every form of new war, NSA spying, the drone killings and other matters, people, even if they did not agree fully, would acknowledge the truth of what we were saying.

The leading edge of what we were doing was warning them that there was a war being planned against the Russians, and the Chinese, and that

This is the moral opposite of Obama: Beauty demonstrates what humankind is that gives us cause to "Stand Up and Fight for Humanity." Here the Schiller Institute New York City Community Chorus performs Handel's Messiah on March 27, 2016 in Brooklyn.

this could not be allowed. We told them that the reason behind the war tensions, was that the U.S. now produces only drug addicts, unemployment, and despair—and they knew this was true.

This did not dissuade the individual who objected to the "Jail Obama" sign. He organized two other people to help remove us from the area. An organizer, however, showed him a picture of Trump morphing into Hillary Clinton with the caption: "What Difference Does It Make?" He burst out laughing when he saw the picture, and he totally changed. He ended up signing the anti-NATO petition, giving $5, and taking the picture down to the corner copy shop so that he could make copies. He took our picture from the table, went to make copies, and then brought our original back.

Finally, on Manhattan's Columbus Circle—a far cry from the South Bronx—an LPAC rally took the form of an amplified Socratic dialogue. The 18 members of the organizing squad were constantly engaged in conversations, distributing literature and organizing people to sign a petition—the petition that the Schiller Institute is circulating in Europe, calling on governments to stop the confrontation being instigated at this moment by NATO on the border of Russia, and orient toward the win-win cooperation proposed by the BRICS. "More foreign troops are massed on the Russian border now than at any time since the Second World War, and you don't even know it!" Scores of people signed the petition, but, more important, 200 people took the petition to circulate it themselves, or to consider it despite their initial doubts about what the organizers were saying.

In this way, LaRouche organizers have *attacked and sought to remove the slave mentality that paralyzes Americans in the face of their fear of the Obama killing machine.*

In day-to-day organizing by members of the LaRouche Political Action Committee— and in particular since the commencement of the 2015-2016 electoral season and Presidential campaign—obsessive-compulsive statements purporting to have something to do with politics had for months been epidemic in encounters with the citizen on the street, that is, until recently. Several factors, including the recent, merciful ending of the "primary season" have changed that. The persistence of Vladimir Putin in Russia, in fighting against terrorism, and in inviting Obama and the United States to join him and work with him, is one such factor. The compelling initiatives of China in space exploration and China's win-win policy for global economic development is another. For the people of the United States, the path toward sanity has been demonstrated by the Manhattan Project.

The Truth Appears

Twenty years ago Lyndon LaRouche said of Obama's ancestors, George Herbert Walker Bush and Margaret Thatcher, the originator of the 1979 Afghanistan War with Russia:

> Shakespeare's Hamlet said: "Murder, though it have no tongue, will speak …" Let Thatcher, Bush, and their accomplices now tremble: Truth appears, and no more weapon than truth itself, will render to the memories of these pirates, the dramatic justice of which William Shakespeare wrote.

The 28 pages suppressed by Obama, and Bush-Cheney before him, *shall speak,* though murder have no tongue.

You Must Lift the Faces of Terrified People, So They Can See Hope!

This is an edited transcript of Lyndon LaRouche's June 11, 2016 dialogue with the Manhattan Project.

Dennis Speed: Lyn, if you would like, give us some opening remarks, and then we'll go right to the Q&A.

Lyndon LaRouche: What is happening is that we have moved some of our action from Manhattan—not to take it away from Manhattan—but in order to bring a broader representation of what Manhattan is saying to the world.

Question: How can we impress on Congress the reality of what's happening now on the borders of Russia? There could be just an accidental push of a button; or it could be a purposeful one by an insane leader in this country. The response from that would lead to a total world war, a total destruction of the planet.

LaRouche: I don't think that problem is of that dimension in this quarter. The point is that there is an international resonance about what the kinds of things that we are speaking about in terms of Manhattan. And I spend a lot of effort and concentration on exactly that. I have several responsibilities now internationally, and one of them is to make sure that the Manhattan organization, which is a leading influence body for the United States, that that body be heard and represented and duly informed.

Question: Hello, Lyn. I have a report and then a question. So, the report is that we have been having a very explosive response from people in the organizing this week. It's been around the whole fight to get out of NATO and to mobilize the American people to even know there's a danger of war, such that we had, for example, long lines of people stopping at a table where we had five organizers. One of our organizers was able to create a debate on this World War III danger. And this really provoked a lot of response from the population to come up and challenge him. So, the population was responding to that.

The question is, this petition is obviously mobilizing a lot of people, and that's good. But we want to know if it is viable for a NATO country to follow our demands? To actually leave NATO before the Warsaw summit happens? And for example, one case is de Gaulle. He pulled his troops out of NATO at one point. So, we wanted to just get a response on that.

LaRouche: I would say that we have to take the responsibility for what the people in the United States *can* and will do. That's the primary consideration. The question then becomes, how will people in other nations of the world also respond to that kind of response? In other words, when people in the United States express and reveal what their views are on the issues facing the United States and beyond, that is what is important for us—is to get a picture of what the American citizen is doing; and what the American citizen is doing by way of thinking, and what decisions are being made.

Now, you know that Manhattan has a history, when the British and the Saudis perpetrated mass murder on the citizens of Manhattan—and I should say that that fact is sufficient to condemn those who continue to tolerate the crimes committed by the President at that time, and by the Saudis and British.

What is the Standard?
Question: Could you say something more about this question of institutional collapses, and the way that the crumbling of institutions actually opens up people's capacity to respond more intelligently to the options that we're presenting? What do you think about this Brexit business? Is this just going to fly by as a news item, or is this…?

LaRouche: No, look, we're talking about an international affair; and people are talking about—oh, some people are talking about this, some people are talking about that, they're talking about different natures about that. Nonsense! *The whole planet is at risk; the entirety of the planet is at risk.* And what we're trying to do is not to save some part of the nation, or nations, but rather, to defend this *national system* from destroying itself. And by taking the measures which will enable that system to defend itself against the kinds of folly that Obama and the British Empire represent.

Question: I wanted to take up with you from a question that Helga responded to earlier in the week, from someone who had some relationship to the organization, had been attending meetings, and was asking Helga to respond to the reality he faces of being chastised, through his association and through his expressing the ideas he picks up from this organization.

And for those people who are coming to us, the whole idea of our cultural work becomes essential, because in Helga's response to this fellow was the idea of developing inner beauty, where you then can know truth, where you want to know truth, and you then can stand up to the silly, stupid neighbors around you, and then eventually, win them over, because you're actually sane and showing some courage. So, around this idea that Helga responded to, we've talked about it a lot. You've talked about it. As we continue our fight, what can you tell us more about this and our work here?

LaRouche: I think it's what Helga, my wife, has done in her time on this issue; and I think the whole nation can be brought into an understanding of this process. What we have to do is lay out how the process works. And then we have to go out and work, and make sure that it does work. We're getting great work from the people in defense of nations at various times; what we're getting is wonderful. I wouldn't worry about that. I think, just do it. Just present the case, identify the case, bring up the key points, and let it go.

Question: My question is returning to the crimes of the Saudis and the British, and the people, including Bush and Obama, who have covered this thing up. When we have discussed this, we have talked about the idea of justice for the victims of 9/11, but the very idea of justice is not well understood in this culture. So my

White House/Pete Souza

President Barack Obama and First Lady Michelle Obama receive Queen Elizabeth II and Prince Philip, Duke of Edinburgh, prior to a dinner in the Queen's honor at Winfield House in London, England, May 25, 2011.

question is: What is this justice that we're seeking; and how could we communicate about that over these next three months as we lead up to the 15th anniversary?

LaRouche: I think that that's too simple, in a sense, because it's much more complicated. The question is, how did people react, to the discovery that a terrible crime is being committed by a major force in some parts of the United States and parts of other nations? That's what the issue is. You have to get not to the point of some issue as such. It's not a local issue. But you have to bring forth what is the standard for the support of the requirements of a human being, or human beings, in order to bring mankind into a more successful form of realization of what mankind is. It's just that simple. I can repeat it in various terms and various ways. But this is not a question of something personal in a simple way. What is the issue of mankind? *Einstein.* Use the word *Einstein.* Don't try to give some other shorthand on it. What Einstein intended, is exactly what you and we should intend....

Use it. It may not be the most perfect expression of the thing, but do it anyway. You need to do something quickly that's going be useful to many people. Do it.

What Defines 'Human'?

Question: Hi, Lyn. What you addressed last week, when Daniel asked his question about "Can genius be taught?"—there was a point in the discussion where you said, "Somebody becomes a genius; and it's not becoming a genius, it's that that quality of genius infects them, they have it. And then, if they are smart, if they are up to living to what they should be, they will express what we call 'genius.'"

And that idea really resonated with me throughout this last week, and we were getting this explosion in the field. But I think it requires not just the potential in the population, but also that we are rising to the challenge of providing that kind of real genius, leadership like Einstein, and not being practical.

So, I wanted to address just this specific point that you made that if people are up to the challenge of living up to that standard. And this is what I see—that when you're tested, then you see really what somebody is made of. And life brings each and every single one of us certain tests. And there's a difference between those exceptional people who rise to the challenge of those tests, and take on the real challenge—emotional, intellectual challenge of leadership.

And what I wanted you to address more was this emotional education... people really having this kind of emotional education, so that when they are tested with the real question of "Am I going to take up leadership at all personal expense for the future of mankind?"

Anyway, I wanted you to really address this question of the emotional education. If Einstein had given in out of fear, if he wasn't totally gripped by these ideas that infected him, if he had given in in any form, we wouldn't have had the great benefits of Einstein. So, I think you get what I'm trying to get at. But we really, we have a lack of that emotional education in people which gives them the courage to not be practical and to be courageous.

LaRouche: Well, I would say, let's shift your choice of character for attention at the moment, not to reject anything about it, but just to simply use a different comparison. Krafft Ehricke. Krafft Ehricke was the founder of about everything: about the Moon, about almost everything. And he was faced with a disease which prevented him from actually dealing with internal conflict,

U.S. Navy/Mass Communication Specialist 1st Class America A. Henry

Included in the four NATO maneuvers taking place in Eastern Europe and the Baltic nations, involving more than 60,000 troops, are U.S. Marines (above) performing a live-fire exercise on June 10, 2016 in Sweden during BALTOPS 2016.

the medical problem,— well he was going to die anyway. He had choices of two ways to live, but what he had was two ways to die. Now, and what he has done, and what he has delivered, and what those who followed him have done, is that. So, while it seems like the naming of a particular person, of being a particular figure, it's not that, but something much more general.

What is the quality, looking at it from the standpoint of Krafft Ehricke's history, what is so sacred about what Krafft Ehricke represented by the time he had died? And that says there's a higher standard of measure which defines the meaning of human; human is not limited to a human person. It is defined in terms of humanity in general; and that's the way to look at it. It works that way.

Question: I want to ask a question that comes up in the organizing. Helga, in her presentation to the San Francisco conference, was clear on the necessity of us presenting internationally, but also to the American people, the absolute danger represented by the war provocations by the NATO drills being done in Eastern Europe, directly provocative to Russia. They're doing drills where you have U.S. armed forces driving from Germany up to Russia's border with the explicit intention of preparing for an ostensible Russian invasion [of the Baltics], which Russia has not announced, or as far as I'm aware, prepared for, or intended to do.

So we've done that. We've had a series of deployments, very high profile with large signs: "Leave NATO." We have this petition, and as I understand it, will continue this initiative, building into the Warsaw summit in a couple of weeks.

I wanted to bring up a question that had come up among some of the organizers, where you had discussed some of these war provocations as "bluffs." That there's a bluff involved with these powers and I want to see if it's a bluff, but it's still a dangerous bluff, how exactly to take this?

LaRouche: It is a dangerous bluff. It *is* a dangerous bluff. The issue is, how will you deal with this bluff? And you can win. We can win, but the point is we have to *not* give in. Because what's happened? Look, the British system, the entire empire, which is the Satan incarnate, essentially, that thing can be defeated! It *is* being defeated! Obama is the major source of complaints on this account. Obama is the best example of pure Satanic motives, himself!

So the point is, the question lies not in who is going to do this, and who is going to do that, as such, although those things have importance. The issue is, what will the American citizen, or the European citizens, do, in terms in response to a Satanic force, like the British Empire, or Obama, who is a real killer?

Look Inside Yourself

Question: My question is coming up to you, because, as an activist in the group, I've noticed a few things, talking to people. First of all, they will sometimes put you off, and the most significant person I talked to, turned out to be this lovely woman who is a physician and has now joined us. And in talking to her, the first thing she said was, "Putin is insane." And I pointed out that Obama is insane. And I asked her things about the NATO provocations, and asked if she knew about them, and asked if she knew the history of Russia and the United States. And I went going through the history of how Russia has never let us down, they've fought with us in several wars—the American Revolution also, the Civil War, and World War II.

And I said, Obama, with his British handlers,

U.S. Air Force/Senior Airman Kenny Holston

This U.S. Air Force B-2 Spirit stealth bomber aircraft was one of several B1-B and B2 bombers that flew missions to destroy Libyan command and control capabilities early in the war against Libya. It is shown here as it returned from a mission against Libya, March 20, 2011.

through NATO are provoking war, and if it's a war, it'll be a nuclear war. And then, she sat and looked at me, and said, "You know, you're right." And I said, "Yes, so you agree? Obama is insane, and Putin is actually just Putin." So she said, "Yeah, that's true." And as I spoke to her, another thing came up, and that was the music. I told her about our music. And, lo and behold, she's going to join us. She's going to come to the conference and deal with the music that we present.

So I just want to bring it to you, and say, can you give a little more insight into what Daniel talking about, and what Michelle was talking about: that truthfulness in us, that comes out when we stick to the truth, and that we can find things out about people, that will actually lead them to even more things like our music?

LaRouche: What you're really dealing with is the fact that there's a popular way in which people commonly interpret social relations. But these things are really not crucial. They can be pesky, a terrible nuisance, but they are not essential to mankind. What is important is what mankind can find in mankind's own self. Now, that's not such a tough job; it is a tough job in one sense, but if mankind, the individual person, can look into themselves and find the real moral principle inside themselves, a principle on which they would act for the purpose of supporting Manhattan, or any other part of the city, or the world, that's it!

We have to, in ourselves, come to a judgment on what is *right,* what is right about mankind? What are the characteristics that distinguish mankind from the beasts and animals and things of that sort? And that's it.

And when you can get on that, when you can look at a terrified person—and there are many terrified persons all over the world these days—and if you can lift their faces, where they can see a hope, a way of working, we can lead to a solution, that's what you're really shooting for. It's not a doing this, or doing that: The question is, can you yourself find, in yourself, the way in which to bring mankind out of the darkness.

A Process Underway on the Planet

Question: [Elliot Greenspan] Hi Lyn, I want to pose two aspects, interrelated: One is that you have emphasized, in a series of discussions over the last days, that much of your concentration is on institutional change, that you're working to transform institutions. I would be grateful to the extent you want publicly to elaborate on that.

But let me pose the second part and you'll see the connection, which is that we are dealing with the population by and large which is brainwashed here, which is deeply beset by a pervasive, fundamental belief that change happens electorally, or congressionally, or through interest groups, or lobbying, or all of these things that Americans have been fed for a long time. And for a long time, we've not had fundamental change in the right direction in the United States; that has a great deal to do, I think, with that kind of bias, that kind of prejudice, that kind of *conceit,* as to how political change occurs.

You, on the other hand, have developed a process and a commitment to political transformation, based on what you call "the principle of the strategic flank." You referenced, for example, MacArthur. You look at the various initiatives, the Manhattan Project, the choral work here, the 28 Pages, what Kesha's doing, the space initiative, the Silk Road, the NATO initiative—these are flanks. And what I think would be invaluable for all of us, is how you think about and generate such flanking actions as the unique basis on which historic, necessary political change occurs; perhaps that then goes back to your thinking about institutional change in the immediate period ahead.

LaRouche: The immediate thing would be what you're going at indirectly, and also directly at the same time, which is the fact that if you want to understand how mankind can survive despite the kinds of evil which dominate much of the planet right now, you have to look inside yourself, find something inside yourself which is so convincing, by its nature, that you say naturally: "Hey, wait a minute, everything I'm doing is insane!" Because what I'm doing, is I'm doing something which I'm trying to get an advantage for. And I say, No, there are no such things as advantages like that. There are no advantages that exist like *that.* All you can get, is to win. Now, what do we mean by "win"? It means, win—to gain the ability to perform the functions of *human* development.

So therefore, it's not something which is a property of this, a property of that. The question is what you, in yourself, inside yourself, what you really embody. Do you have the ability to *pick up* those values which must be served, for the sake of humanity as a general phenomenon? Without that, you are not armed. You are disarmed.

And I think you won't have any trouble looking through that, and thinking about it, because I know you.

Question: Hi Lyn. I have a question from Avneet, so I'll be reading that to you. The Indian Prime Minister recently visited Washington, D.C. and inspired Americans again, like he did two years ago, when he spoke at Madison Square Garden. In his Congressional speech, he invoked Lincoln and emphasized that we have to be united to fight terrorism.

Westinghouse now plans to build six nuclear power plants in India. Modi also emphasized that India is now a global leader, and he mentioned the projects in Afghanistan and Iran that India is investing in. So overall, you have a completely different, palpable environment in Capitol Hill. What do you think of all this?

LaRouche: I think that there's a process under way in which much of the planet, among nations, wants to do the right thing, so-called. That is, to bring about the kind of conditions of life, as prospects and as realities, which are needed for humanity's existence.

LaRouche stated that building the Kra Canal is probably one of the most important issues for all mankind, now.

That's where I stand. I think there is no other choice which is competent. And what the problem has been, is that we have nations which, like the British or like Obama, who's an evil fellow himself, that these kinds of things, these forms of evil, bring down on mankind generally, but they bring down finally against mankind generally, himself.

Question: Hi, Lyn. You mentioned the Kra Canal in recent discussions, and you said something very specific about it, early in the week about how this would be, for example, if the activity that you began 30 years ago, with the Mitsubishi corporation and associates from Japan, to get this thing built, that this would change the nature of everything. And you re-emphasized that in a different way this week. I thought it might be appropriate to discuss it.

LaRouche: The key thing, the first thing in this light: India. And if India were to open the gates, there, what you would have, you have an immediate change in the entire character of the water systems around the world. Especially the trans-Pacific matter.

So that was there. It's been there all along. There is a tempering now, to go into that, to realize that, to bring it back into reality, the way that Japan did in that period, because Japan was resolved, at first, to keep the Kra Canal program going. They gave up on the idea, but the idea has always persisted. And that Kra Canal operation is probably one of the most important issues for *all mankind,* now.

Question: Hi Lyn. So, I've been doing a lot of work to build the chorus in Brooklyn and in the area, and a thing that I'm running up against is that I do run into a lot of people who are interested in joining it, but then they'll come for a little bit, and then they won't come again. I want to get your thoughts on how we can escalate so that we can build this up, so that by the time in September, we have a major breakthrough.

LaRouche: Well, this is not a mechanical question, and the tendency is to look at this as a mechanical question. "Can we convince this guy to go along with this thing?" Well, that is not the way to do it. The point is that the individual as a musician, the individual musician, is the actual source of the *passion* which motivates creative music, and creative entertainment in general.

So you're not looking for a recipe. You're looking for something *inside yourself,* and you're trying to find out if you have inside *yourself* the kind of thing that will bring you and cause you to present a competent performance! There's no other solution. You have to do it.

'A Whole Different Conception Of Mankind'

This is an edited transcript of Kesha Rogers' presentation to the Schiller Institute's June 8 Strategic Seminar in San Francisco, "Will the United States Join the New Silk Road?"

Kesha Rogers, the La-Rouche PAC Policy Committee leader based in Houston, Texas, was twice elected the Democratic Party nominee for the Congressional District that includes the Houston Space Center. She is leading the campaign for the revival of the U.S. Space Program shut down by Barack Obama.

I'm here and we're going to talk!

It was a blessing when Mr. LaRouche asked me to lead the campaign to revive the Space Program, because the Space Program is at the heart of our nation's potential contribution to the world, once we choose to return to space, as we must.

I agree with what Helga Zepp-LaRouche said at the beginning of her presentation: There is currently *no* discussion of the war policy which threatens the extinction of mankind. It must be addressed now. I also agree with Senator Gravel, who said earlier that Obama's military provocations and his drive towards war threaten our very existence.

That also gets to the question of where the policy of shutting down NASA has come from. I ran for Congress against Obama's destruction of our Space Pro-

EIRNS/Stuart Lewis
Space scientist Krafft Ehricke addressing a 1981 meeting.

gram. But why is it that now, none of the presidential candidates, even Sen. Bernie Sanders, has the policy that we as a nation must resume mankind's mission in space? We must reject the compromises which have been made with this President and his policy of dismantling the Space Program; we must recognize that that policy is a threat to human existence itself. The fact of the matter is, that not only do these Presidential candidates not have a space policy, but that they have continued to capitulate to President Obama's policy of war, and to capitulate to President Obama's policy of *not* collaborating with nations which represent the interest of who we are as a human species, particularly in space exploration.

Krafft Ehricke

Mr. LaRouche has long understood this: What we need right now is a transformation of our identity as a human species, and the best way to achieve that is through the understanding of mankind's role in the exploration and conquest of space. Now, what the Space Program represents is not just the technological aspect, not just the development of new technologies, but it gets at the very philosophy that governs the fabric of our human existence. It is important to make that point clear. I know that there are a people here today who have very technical backgrounds, and who are probably more competent in various scientific aspects of the Space Program than I am. But what I would like to offer in this dialogue and discussion, is what has been lost in the shutdown of the Space Program from the standpoint of what the great German space pioneer, Krafft Ehricke, contributed.

Why is it that Krafft Ehricke was a great collaborator of ours, and someone who became very close to Mr. LaRouche and Mr. LaRouche's thinking,— and to our movement's thinking concerning the policy that governs the understanding of space exploration? Indeed, it governs not just space exploration, but the destiny of who we are as a species, as mankind. We have accepted a system of limitations imposed on mankind; in reality, there are no limitations to be imposed on mankind.

Krafft Ehricke was a German scientist who came to the United States and worked as part of Operation Paperclip, with scientists such as Wernher von Braun and others who had worked on the V-2 rocket in Germany.

Now, what is fascinating about Ehricke, is that he did not believe in or accept the conditions of being "practical" or of doing that which is acceptable, per se. He had a different concept, a different philosophy to understand and govern the relationships among nations, peoples, and the cosmos and the Solar system as a whole. He put forward the conception of nations moving from their understanding of the limitations of a single planet, a one-globe planet, to a "polyglobal" world. Now if we are going to defend ourselves as nations, as human beings, we have to look at what Russia, China, and other nations are doing to initiate what Krafft Ehricke understood as the emergence of a poly-global world, as our destiny in a world that expands out into the outer reaches of our Solar System, and that actually rejects the limitations imposed on mankind.

Ehricke understood, first of all, what would lead to a society which accepts dictatorship, a society which accepts chauvinistic policies in the political realm, or a society that accepts the dismantling of nations, or nations being divided. He saw that there were two opposing views of society. One he called an "open-world" conception of mankind, which rejects limitations imposed on mankind, while the other view was what he called a "closed-world" conception. I'll discuss these in just a moment. He understood this also because he lived through those conditions in World War II Germany, and also understood why some *accepted* the policies of fascism under Hitler.

Krafft Ehricke's identity was really formed when, as a child, at the age of twelve, he was introduced to the work of the great German space pioneer and scientist Hermann Oberth. He also saw Fritz Lang's movie "The Woman in the Moon," and this completely transformed his life.

He studied aeronautical engineering at Technological University of Berlin in 1938. He was drafted and sent to France. There he was run over by a tank, and had his leg broken in several places. Back in Berlin to recover, he continued his studies in engineering, and continued to promote, even through the horrors of Nazism and war, the importance of the exploration of space, where mankind would soon go.

After recovering, he was sent to Russia, in a tank unit. But what happened was that in 1942, because of the papers he was publishing on rocket design and some of his other works, he was called to work with von Braun and others at the Peenemünde V-2 rocket facility.

Later, Krafft Ehricke learned that his entire unit had been wiped out in Russia. Much of what we accomplished in space, and much of what we will accomplish in the future, would probably not have happened if he had stayed in Russia to be killed with the rest of his unit.

I find him very remarkable because, despite all this, when the first team of scientists was sent to the United States, to Fort Bliss, Texas, he declined to go. This was right after the war. He declined because he had a wife in Berlin. He was in Bavaria at the time. He walked for 30 days because, remember, all the infrastructure had been wiped out,— 30 days to the capital, Berlin, to find his wife. After that, they left for the U.S.

A Fight Worth Fighting

That history is relevant, because the determination of a human mind, the determination of a single individual to make such contributions, points to our creative potential as human beings to overcome any obstacles and to fight for that which is truly human; and that's what Krafft Ehricke represents. That's what our organization, and what Mr. LaRouche has continued to fight for.

What Ehricke made clear, was his understanding of the importance of his conception of space exploration, which has to be the model for why we fight on for the development of space: It is not simply for the sake of

FIGURE 1

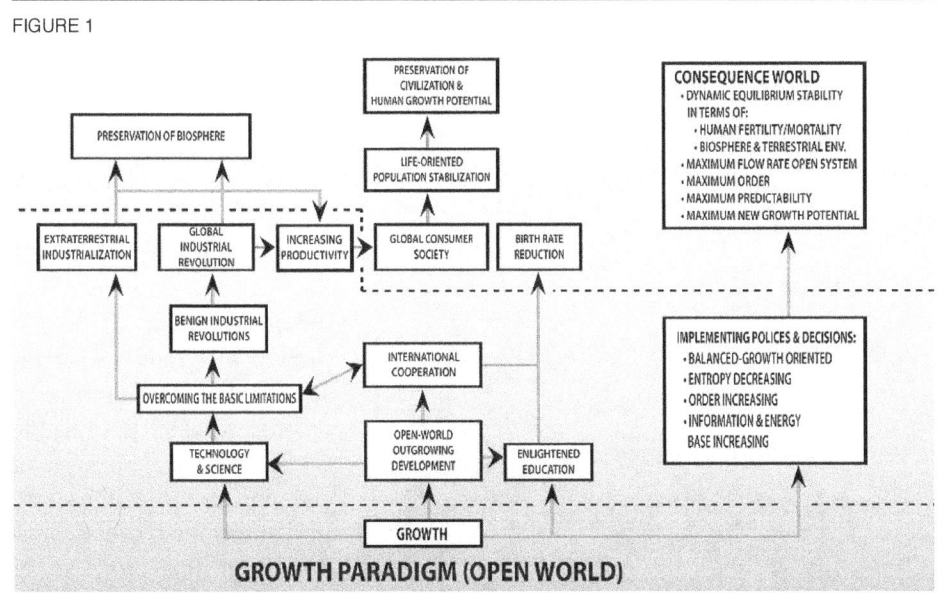

GROWTH PARADIGM (OPEN WORLD)

the technological advances, although they are useful; but he had a different idea.

Here is an example. Ehricke wrote: "The concept of space travel carries with it enormous impact, because it challenges man on practically all fronts of his physical and spiritual existence. The idea of travelling to other celestial bodies reflects to the very highest degree the independence and agility of the human mind. It lends ultimate dignity to man's technical and scientific endeavors. Above all, it touches on the philosophy of his very existence. As a result, the concept of space travel disregards national borders, refuses to recognize differences of historical or ethnological origins, and penetrates the fiber of one sociological or political creed as fast as that of the next."

I think that what we are seeing right now points towards the emergence of a new conception of mankind, a new era, a new paradigm for mankind represented by what Russia and China are doing, which half of humanity is now moving toward. It is the only choice, the only option that we have right now for a renewed conception of who we are as a species. *None of this political stuff is going to suffice.* No other lower conception will suffice.

Today's trans-Atlantic system lurching towards war under British Empire puppet Obama, stands for a no-growth policy, and for crippling limitations imposed on mankind. Contrast that with the open-world system which Krafft Ehricke defines as the removal of limitations. With that we can actually take the economic expansion that we are seeing right now centered in Eur-

asia, and not only spread that for expansion throughout the world, but throughout our Solar System as well.

So, let's take a look at this for a second, because the philosophy of a closed world system has been a dominant one, but now that dominant philosophy is under attack and is being removed. **[Figure 1]**

This is the debate that is well worth having right now in any sort of political setting, whether Democratic, Republican, or whatever. This is the question of the human debate over who we are, and what our mission and destiny as a human species is. It is this which connects all of us, whatever our backgrounds, to a better understanding of what our contributions to the future of mankind must be. We must ask what are going to be the contributions we make to those future generations, those children not yet born; we must ask and study and find the answers. This mission must replace the present trans-Atlantic system headed for the annihilation of all humanity through thermonuclear war.

I've had my handy associate, my husband, put together these charts for me: These are charts which are enhanced from Ehricke's work, from a schematic that he made in the 1970s, on the principle of a growth versus no-growth world, open-world versus closed-world system. If you think about the growth paradigm: It rejects the view of society based on limits to growth imposed on mankind, and actually rejects the entropic worldview. You can also see that it's moving upwards in terms of developments around advances in technology and advances in global society, looking towards what we would call a maximum open-world system.

It's fascinating, because Ehricke was really forecasting what was to come, in terms of the acceptance of a society of bestiality, of chauvinistic views, of geopolitical policies, and all the rest of what he understood were the poisonous consequences of the Club of Rome's no-growth policy. This is not the nature of who we are as a human species.

FIGURE 2

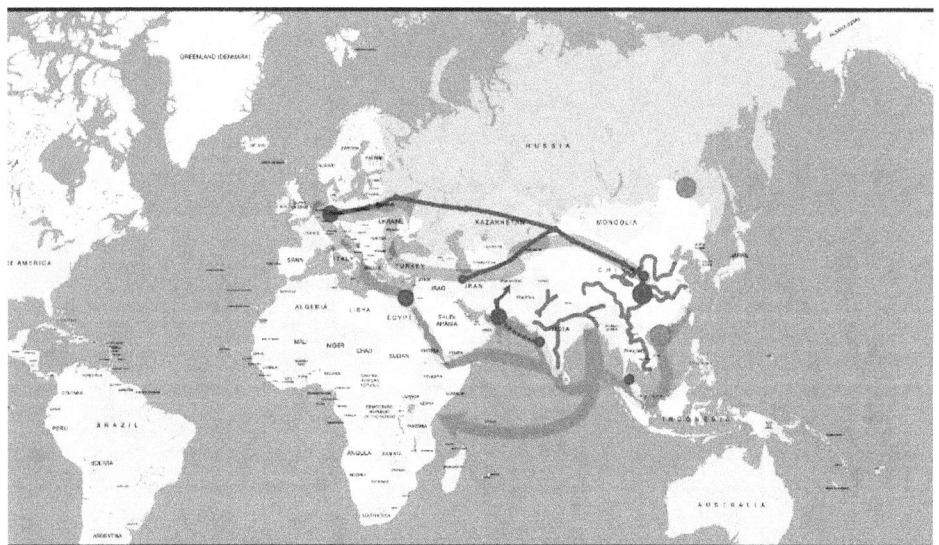

And also, he forecast [**Figure 2**] what we see as the move into a polyglobal world, which is being led by Russia and China. What you see here are the consequences of a growth paradigm. This growth paradigm today is the emergence of the 40-year fight of Mr. and Mrs. LaRouche around the Silk Road development plan, and the policy for space exploration. The travel to the far side of the Moon will become a new, total transformation of mankind in the coming two years, when China reaches that goal, never accomplished before.

paradigm that rejects the limitations that have been imposed on mankind. Now on the other side, Ehricke knew what would happen if we didn't move in that direction. [**Figure 3**] These are the consequences of a no-growth system, of a no-growth paradigm which insists that there are limited resources, which accepts the winding-down of our system, and the idea that there are limitations that can be imposed on the progress of mankind.

He made this very clear. If you look at this, you see that this is exactly where we are today in the trans-Atlantic system, under the policies promoted by the British and promoted by President Obama. If you accept this no-growth paradigm, the results will be extreme poverty, mass starvation, and wars. This is what we see in the NATO escalation and provocations toward war on the Baltic Sea, and what we are seeing in the South China Sea. Ehricke was right on the mark in his understanding of what happens to a society that allows for the elimination of our creative identity as a species, and ac-

Opportunities Before Us

I won't go through all of these projects. The two red dots are Russia's and China's new space launch centers; the long purple line there that goes from China to Duisburg, Germany, is the rail connection and corridors of development there; you have also the development around the South-North Water Projects of China in the blue there; and also the development of the Chabahar Port in Iran, involving India and Afghanistan.

This, then, is the growth

FIGURE 3

NO-GROWTH PARADIGM (CLOSED WORLD)

FIGURE 4

cepts geopolitical and other policies that say that human beings are nothing more than beasts.

This closed-world system, at this very moment, is being rejected by Russia and China and their allies. [**Figure 4**] Think of the development plans being furthered by Russia and China, India, and throughout the world, including the water development projects, the projects for high-speed rail systems, and the expansion into space exploration. Think why it is that that represents a threat to the no-growth policies that we're seeing here. Think in this connection of the hotspots of provocations of war. And these are just a few—but you get the picture: If you took that other growth map, and what we're seeing in these development plans, and put this on top of it, you know why that represents a threat to the empire's drive toward a war of extinction and annihilation, and why this has to be stopped now.

How Will We Do It?

I think we have a great potential and opportunity before us. I want to look very directly and clinically at why Mrs. LaRouche said that the absence of the discussion of the threat imposed on mankind cannot be accepted,— because until we discuss this threat, we will not be able to solve the problem. We must activate our human ability to transcend this threat to mankind's very existence. And we have the potential to do that. We have the potential to actually take mankind to a new level of cooperation that has long been forgotten.

That's what we are seeing right now, and it requires the renewed creativity of who we are as human beings, of who we are in terms of our understanding of what we have to bring about for the future.

If you look at what it is that we have to create, it means that we have to look into the future right now, and most people don't have that conception any longer, because they've lost a sense of our creative identity. We're thinking about the "now,"— how do I survive? What am I going to survive on? How am I going to make my next paycheck? But Ehricke had a different idea about mankind: that the threat of starvation, and all of what we're facing right now,— all of what people think are unsolvable problems on Earth,— are absolutely solvable, if we come together around an understanding of our extraterrestrial imperative as a species. Then we can solve these problems by rejecting the limitations that have been imposed on us, as we go out into our destiny in space.

This is an artist's painting from a drawing by Ehricke of a Moon colony. [**Figure 5**] It's interesting that recently there's been a lot of discussion related to this. At a recent conference, the head of the European Space Agency made the point of the importance of mankind going out into space, and said that we have to develop villages on the Moon and that our destiny is the colonization of Mars. This is also something that is being discussed right now by the Chinese, who want to send astronauts to the Moon by 2036. It is something that China and Russia are working on in collaboration, and other nations around the world are pursuing.

You ask, "How are we going to do that?" Well, we're going to do that because we're going to vastly increase what we can do to solve the problems here on Earth, by understanding the resources that exist within our Solar System,— such as the development of helium-3 on the Moon, which is a very important resource to develop for fusion power. [**Figure 6**] This is a

FIGURE 5

Courtesy of Krafft Ehricke

Selenopolis, a city on the Moon, as envisioned by Krafft Ehricke. At left is the Hall of Astronauts museum, Note the indoor monorail for getting around in the city. Ehricke's concept of the Moon was as Earth's 'Seventh Continent.'

FIGURE 6

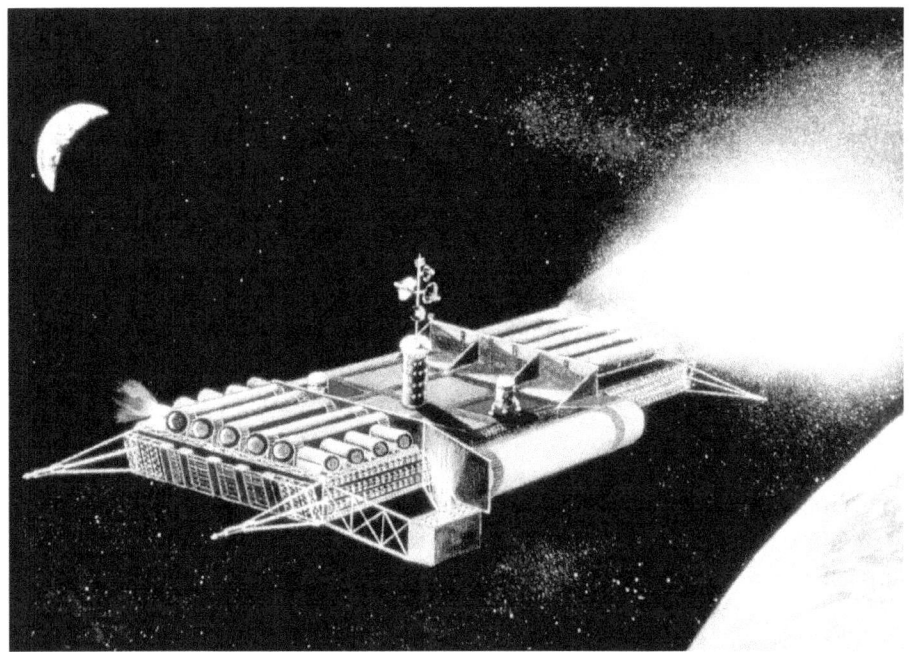

Courtesy of Krafft Ehricke

This nuclear powered lunar freighter uses materials on the Moon for fuel. It is one of the vehicles Ehricke designed as part of the transportation infrastructure that would open the solar system to mankind.

lunar freighter that would allow for bringing different resources to the Moon. A flotilla of vehicles will go to the Moon, to develop the Moon, and develop the resources on the Moon that will allow us to expand on to Mars and other planetary bodies.

Now Ehricke was a pioneer of new chemical fuels for rockets; most important was the liquid hydrogen fuel of the Centaur rocket which was critical to the U.S. Space Program. But he had realized as early as the 1940s, that our exploration into space was going to have to be done through developing nuclear power resources.

So, he had a creative imagination that took the mind of man out of the swamp which says that we cannot solve these problems, and that we must impose limitations on ourselves; because he made very clear that the philosophy of man rejects this conception, the philosophy of our human species rejects this conception.

What eliminates the conflicts which pit nation against nation and family against family, is mankind's collaboration around the development of space exploration. You just think about it: There on the Moon there's not going to be a territory for Russia, a territory for China, a territory for India, and so forth. There are not going to be nuclear weapons on the Moon. There's going to be a whole different conception of mankind. And that's something that people can't even imagine now, because we've become so accepting of

FIGURE 7

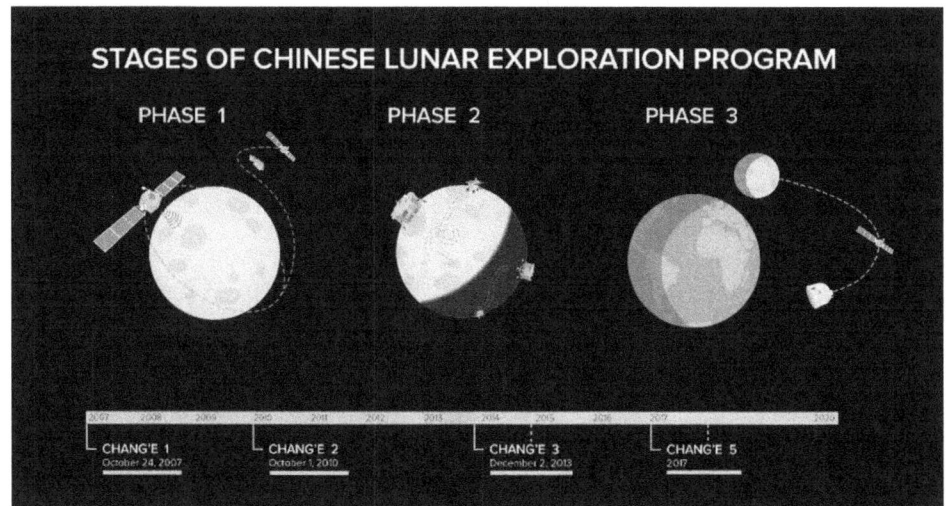

STAGES OF CHINESE LUNAR EXPLORATION PROGRAM

PHASE 1   PHASE 2   PHASE 3

CHANG'E 1
October 24, 2007

CHANG'E 2
October 1, 2010

CHANG'E 3
December 2, 2013

CHANG'E 5
2017

this closed-world system, of this one-world system, that we have lost sight of the fact that our human species has a destiny!

And that destiny can only be understood through the spark within us that is the reason we fight for a Space Program, that spark which is the reason that we now have the opportunity to put an end, once and for all, to the geopolitical view of the world, which has brought us almost to the annihilation of mankind. [**Figure 7**]

I hope I have given you something to think about. We have the opportunity to overcome these challenges, if we choose to do the right thing, which is located in our conception of what is going to unify us as a species, what's going to develop and expand our human species to a level that has never been known before. I think Russia and China, and the nations joining them, are ready to do that, and have made a commitment to do that. The question is whether the American people, whether you are ready to do that.

The Power of Truth Can Overthrow the Russellite Dictatorship!

by David Christie and Robert Ingraham

June 12—Those engaged in the political battle to stop the current NATO war drive, face a serious problem when they attempt to mobilize Americans around a perspective for war avoidance and global economic recovery. The organizers often despair over the apparent refusal of citizens to engage in rational dialogue, citizens who seem to cling ferociously to their "personal opinions," no matter what contrary evidence is presented to them.

The frustrated political organizer may not realize that the problem lies not with a phenomenon of individual opinions, but rather with carefully developed methods of social control that have their origins in the years before World War II and that have now achieved sophisticated deployment in the age of Facebook, Twitter, and Instagram. What vast numbers of people insist are their own personal opinions, their own personal beliefs, are in fact, the product of carefully orchestrated techniques of group control, networking and manipulation.

In his book, *The Impact of Science on Society*, Bertrand Russell stated,

> I think the subject which will be of most importance politically is Mass Psychology ... Education should aim at destroying free will, so that, after pupils have left school, they shall be incapable, throughout the rest of their lives, of thinking or acting otherwise than as their schoolmasters would have wished ...

> The social psychologists of the future will have a number of classes of school children on whom they will try different methods of producing an unshakable conviction that snow is black ... The opinion that snow is white must be held to show a morbid taste for eccentricity ... It is for future scientists to make these maxims precise and discover exactly how much it costs per head to make children believe that snow is black, and how much less it would cost to make them believe it is dark gray. The populace will not be allowed to know how its convictions were generated. When the technique has been perfected, every government that has been in charge of education for more than one generation will be able to control its subjects securely without the need of armies or policemen.

Today, the implementation of Russell's recipe for an oligarchical state is far advanced within the culture of the trans-Atlantic world as a result of the now almost universal use of techniques known as *Social Network Analysis* and *Sociomapping*. Such social control mechanisms have several separate but related goals. Among these are the broad manipulation of popular opinion

youtube grab from Will Durant

Human creative thought was the enemy for Lord Bertrand Russell, above.

President Obama (left) conferring with Ben Rhodes, Deputy National Security Adviser for Strategic Communications, in the Oval Office.

for by the Wolfowitz Doctrine and the related Project for a New American Century—under the banner of fighting Muslim Terrorists, would lead to regional wars and an eventual global nuclear confrontation with Russia, China, and India.

The post-9/11 coup was then used to shift towards a "unitary executive," systematically icing out the institution of the Presidency—especially the influence of LaRouche. The use of the press, and increasingly the use of social media, has been instrumental in bypassing the institution of the Presidency. Under Obama, the British Empire has consolidated the use of these tools in a way that has never been done before and has also fundamentally altered the nature of the U.S. government itself.

Much of the story of what was done, first under George W. Bush but then far more extensively under Barack Obama, was described by Ben Rhodes, Obama's Deputy National Security Adviser for Strategic Communications, in a May 5 *New York Times Magazine* article by David Samuels titled, "The Aspiring Novelist Who Became Obama's Foreign-Policy Guru: How Ben Rhodes rewrote the rules of diplomacy for the digital age." In the article, Rhodes describes the modern, integrated use of a variety of media outlets and social media to enforce Obama's fascist agenda through coercion and manipulation, or "nudging" in the words of the behaviorist Cass Sunstein.

In the *New York Times Magazine* article, Samuels points to an exchange with Leon Panetta, who was Secretary of Defense in Obama's first term, to demonstrate how this process functioned:

In Panetta's telling, his own experience at the Pentagon under Obama sometimes resembled being installed in the driver's seat of a car and finding that the steering wheel and brakes had been disconnected from the engine. Obama and his aides used political elders like him, Robert Gates, and Hillary Clinton as cover to end the Iraq war, and then decided to steer their own course.

and "accepted" ways of thinking; the political deployment of such methods, including through "color revolutions" and the recent overthrow of Brazilian President Dilma Rousseff; and the identification of those individuals and leaders who represent a threat to the trans-Atlantic Empire. Those individuals and leaders, who are labeled *Cognitive Generators*—that is, those who are able to "deploy others around ideas"—are then targeted as threats to be discredited and destroyed.

I. Obama's Echo Chamber

After the terrorist attacks of September 11, 2001, Lyndon LaRouche was virtually the only figure of prominence in the United States to state the truth about what had happened, having forecast the events of September 11 nine months earlier when he warned that the Bush Administration would orchestrate a "Reichstag Fire." LaRouche was also one of the very few voices within the institution of the Presidency to take on the ensuing war drive, which he had also forecast in 1999 in his "Storm over Asia" video presentation. That video described how the launching of small wars—as called

DOD/R.D. Ward

Former Secretary of Defense Leon Panetta found that Obama did not care what foreign policy professionals thought.

While Panetta pointedly never mentions Rhodes's name, it is clear whom he is talking about.

"There were staff people who put themselves in a position where they kind of assumed where the president's head was on a particular issue, and they thought their job was not to go through this open process of having people present all these different options, but to try to force the process to where they thought the president wanted to be," he says. "They'd say, 'Well, this is where we want you to come out.' And I'd say '[expletive], that's not the way it works. We'll present a plan, and then the president can make a decision.' I mean, Jesus Christ, it is the president of the United States; you're making some big decisions here; he ought to be entitled to hear all of those viewpoints and not to be driven down a certain path."

Whether Panetta believes Obama was responsible for a reckless approach to deliberation on foreign policy or not, is irrelevant. Panetta's account of the process indicates that Obama does not care what professionals from the foreign policy establishment, and the institution of the Presidency more generally, actually think. This has also been corroborated by many other accounts. Obama doesn't care, because Obama's policies are determined by the British Crown and its lackeys.

The echo chamber of press and social media is then used to bypass the institutions and generate support from the *vox populi*. Again, from the Samuels article:

"We created an echo chamber," Ben Rhodes admitted, when I asked him to explain the onslaught of freshly minted experts cheerleading for the Iran nuclear deal. *"They were saying things that validated what we had given them to say."* Rhodes goes on to further elaborate the policy of Obama to confuse the American people. He discusses the fact that most of the newspapers no longer have foreign bureaus, and that the young reporters in their late 20s call the White House to get an explanation of "what's happening in Moscow and Cairo." *"They literally know nothing."*

"And we're going to map it onto what we know about the different audiences we're dealing with: the public, pundits, experts, the right wing, Congress." By applying 21st-century data and networking tools to the white-glove world of foreign affairs, the White House was able to track what United States senators and the people who worked for them, and influenced them, were seeing online—and make sure that no potential negative comment passed without a tweet.

Narratives

In addition to using these tools to bypass the institution of the Presidency, these modern mind-benders also use tools to create the "narrative" for Barack Obama that allows him to escape any penalty for his crimes, and gain "support" from the American people to justify his agenda.

One narrative is that it is Vladimir Putin who is "insane," a dictator who is leading the world to World War III. Social scientists, such as Ben Rhodes, other social networkers, mathematicians, and psychologists carefully create a "narrative" that validates such an analysis. Articles are placed in newspapers, websites, blogs, and social media. Then a stable of "commentators" responds to the original postings, and then others respond to them. An artificially created "dialogue" suddenly appears in hundreds of locations. It is fine-tuned for each targeted group. It is carefully monitored, and the responses and number of "hits" logged and studied.

The process is tweaked; "nodal points" of difficulty are identified, and suddenly the narrative is treated as reality.

The end result is that every action taken by Obama to lead the world closer and closer to nuclear war is justified by the "evidence" manufactured in the "evil Putin" narrative.

Methods of attack are devised to ridicule or isolate those who disagree with the narrative. For example, those who point out the lack of evidence for manmade "global warming" are labeled as "deniers," that is, practically pro-Nazi criminals; or those who identify the Saudi-British authorship of the 9/11 attacks are threatened that they may be fingered as "9/11 truthers" or "conspiracy nuts." Again, such slanders are scrupulously placed in key locations on the Internet and in social media for maximum effect. Thousands, even millions, of people repeat these mantras without realizing that they are victims of a system that enforces a conformity of thought.

One such narrative is that it is impossible to remove Obama from office, even though word of his participation in the ongoing coverup of the British-Saudi role in 9/11 is breaking out around the world and the evidence of Obama's backing for terrorists in Syria is now a matter of public record. People simply accept the conclusion that Obama cannot be removed because "that's what everyone says."

Consensus is maintained through group dynamics and people's fear of being alienated from their peer group. Those who do not submit to the "democracy" of consensus will be targeted and infiltrated with tactics to sow cognitive dissonance. A prime tactic is the use of fear—fear of social alienation, fear of reprisal through loss of income or job opportunities, or simply physical fear for one's safety.

Cognitive Infiltration

In an April 2009 webcast, LaRouche delivered his psychological assessment of Barack Obama, warning that he suffered from clinical narcissism like the Emperor Nero. He explained that like Nero, Obama would eliminate all of his advisers except a small inner core known as the "behaviorists." Cass Sunstein, a leading behaviorist, and his wife Samantha Power, the Ambassador to the United Nations, were in that inner core. Sunstein's book *Nudge* makes the case for manipulating

creative commons/Mathew W. Hutchins, Harvard Law Review

In 2009 Lyndon LaRouche said that narcissist Obama would eliminate all his advisers except for a small inner core of "behaviorists." Cass Sunstein, above, is part of that inner behaviorist core.

people based on their base motives—their fear of pain and their pursuit of pleasure. However, those who could not be manipulated into conformity or who could not accept the consensus, would be targeted. In a 2008 paper entitled "Conspiracy Theories," which Sunstein coauthored with Adrian Vermeule, discusses the danger that the pursuit of truth poses to a fascist police state. This is stated fairly clearly in the final paragraph of the paper:

Some conspiracy theories create serious risks. They do not merely undermine democratic debate; in extreme cases, they create or fuel violence. If government can dispel such theories, it should do so. One problem is that its efforts might be counterproductive, because efforts to rebut conspiracy theories also legitimate them. We have suggested, however, that government can minimize this effect by rebutting more rather than fewer theories, by enlisting independent groups to supply rebuttals, and by *cognitive infiltration* designed to break up the crippled epistemology of conspiracy minded groups and informationally isolated social networks.

Sunstein discusses those organizations with "crippled" epistemology, and the need to cognitively infiltrate them and spread *cognitive diversity*. A key example of cognitive infiltration and cognitive diversity is to be found in the ongoing efforts of the Obama administration to cover up the truth of what actually occurred in the attacks on September 11, 2001—the political Achilles' heel of the British Monarchy that stands behind Obama.

Recently, the danger of an "infectious" idea was demonstrated by the recent activities of former U.S. Senator Bob Graham, in his campaign to reveal the truth about the Saudi authorship of the 9/11 attacks. His recent interview in the widely viewed German WDR TV program "Monitor" has sparked a slew of articles in Germany and beyond.

Sunstein and his ilk attempt to counteract the impact of what Senator Graham is doing by inundating conspiracy blogs and so-called "patriot" websites with alternate "narratives" that "Israel was responsible for 9/11," or that the U.S. government brought down the towers in Manhattan with "shaped explosives," or that "a missile hit the Pentagon"—all of this designed to confuse and demoralize people as part of Sunstein's "cognitive diversity" infiltration. In this

Kurt Lewin of the London Tavistock Institute was one of the theorists of cognitive confusion.

way, anyone who disagrees with the official Bush/Obama fairy tale can be labeled as a kook, and all discussion of the strategic implications of the attacks, or how to situate them within the larger domain of what LaRouche discussed in his "Storm over Asia" video, is effectively neutralized.

Sunstein even has the chutzpah to quote Philip Zelikow on the 9/11 "conspiracies." Zelikow was the Bush Administration plant as executive director of the 9/11 Commission, and worked to prevent people on the commission from gaining access to the 28 Pages of the Joint Congressional Inquiry. Zelikow centralized everything around himself, forbade any direct contact between the staff and the ten Commissioners, and reduced the latter almost to the status of figureheads. Worse, Zelikow was later found to be maintaining a secret back channel to the Bush White House, with fre-

quent calls with Karl Rove and Condoleezza Rice. Sunstein writes,

> Philip Zelikow, the Executive Director of the 9/11 commission, says that "the hardcore conspiracy theorists are totally committed. They'd have to repudiate much of their life identity in order not to accept some of that stuff. That's not our worry. Our worry is when things become infectious … then this stuff can be deeply corrosive to public understanding. You can get where the bacteria can sicken the larger body."

II. From Sociometry to Social Network Analysis

The tactic of "cognitive diversity" is not a new concept. The London Tavistock Institute's Kurt Lewin, later the father of the concept of *Group Dynamics*, discusses how to create mental paralysis with this cognitive dissonance. Lewin wrote in 1942,

> One of the main techniques for breaking morale through a 'strategy of terror' consists in exactly this tactic—keep the person hazy as to where he stands and just what he may expect. If in addition frequent vacillations between severe disciplinary measures and promises of good treatment together with spreading of contradictory news, make the 'cognitive structure' of this situation utterly unclear, then the individual may cease to even know when a particular plan would lead toward or away from his goal. Under these conditions even those who have definite goals and are ready to take risks, will be paralyzed by severe inner conflicts in regard to what to do.[1]

1. Kurt Lewin, "Time Perspective and Morale," in Goodwin Watson (ed.), *Civilian Morale*, second yearbook of the Society for the Psychological Study of Social Issues (SPSSI), Boston: Houghton Mifflin, 1942.

When someone is "paralyzed by severe inner conflicts in regard to what to do," he or she is extremely susceptible to behavior modification, or "brainwashing." The Tavistock Institute is one of the key agencies used by the British Monarchy to consciously deploy techniques to induce this paralysis on a mass scale.

In 1937 Jacob Moreno, later the originator of the psychodrama method, founded *Sociometry: A Journal of Interpersonal Relations*. Over the next decades it published articles by John Dewey of Columbia University, George Gallup of the American Institute of Public Opinion (known for its Gallup Poll), Frank Stanton (later of CBS), anthropologist Margaret Mead, Kurt Lewin, Paul Lazarsfeld, Gordon Allport, and Theodore Adorno of the Frankfurt School, among others.

Moreno's psychodrama method is often described as therapy through play-acting, although Moreno would push the limits of the concept. For example, he organized a psychodrama session in which a suicidal woman went through the steps of acting out her own suicide, with other actors playing the part of nurses, all the way up to the moment before her final step.

The core group around *Sociometry* made up the bulk of the staff of the Radio Research Project, funded by the Rockefeller Foundation, supposedly to look into the effects of mass media on society, but actually to run experiments in large-scale behavior modification. Paul Lazarsfeld was the director. Gordon Allport, one of Tavistock's top operatives in the United States, was Lazarsfeld's assistant. Theodore Adorno was music director. Frank Stanton, who went on to become the head of CBS after World War II, was also part of the project.

In 1938, the Radio Research Project carried out one of its most famous operations, Orson Welles narrating H.G. Wells' "War of the Worlds" on Halloween. Given the growing threat of fascism, and the rumblings of war, it is not surprising that many Americans who heard that broadcast did not immediately think there was the invasion of aliens—they thought there was an invasion of Nazis. In an important way they were right. The heirs of *Sociometry* would ultimately provide the foundation for the present, integrated front of modern fascism that deploys opinion research polls, mass media, academia, and eventually social media.

The intellectual heirs of Jacob Moreno and others at *Sociometry* would eventually form the core of the International Network of Social Network Analysis (INSNA) in 1977. INSNA created the social network analysis software that would be used to monitor and profile today's social media sites such as Facebook.

INSNA's current website states:

Network analysis is based on the intuitive notion that these patterns are important features of the lives of the individuals who display them. Network analysts believe that how an individual lives depends in large part on how that individual is tied into the larger web of social connections. Many believe, moreover, that the success or failure of societies and organizations often depends on the patterning of their internal structure.

That kind of intuition is probably as old as humankind. It is implied, for example, by the relative stress put on descent lists in the Bible. And, beginning in the 1930s, a systematic approach to theory and research, based on that notion, began to emerge. In 1934 Jacob Moreno introduced the ideas and tools of sociometry. And at the end of World War II, Alex Bavelas founded the Group Networks Laboratory at M.I.T.

In addition to the seasoned veterans of the Radio Research Project associated with *Sociometry*, INSNA also drew on veterans of the British Empire's colonial program in Africa, namely sociologists and anthropologists around the Rhodes-Livingstone Institute (RLI, founded 1938), whose key informal patron was Lord Malcolm Hailey of the "Milner Group" that had originated with Lord Milner's Round Table. The anthropologists and sociologists of the RLI mapped out the social networks and relationships of the "natives," using Moreno's sociograms, to manipulate them into a democratic consensus suitable for the colonial operations of the British Empire. INSNA became a kind of clearing house that included elements of the British colonial operations of the RLI, Jacob Moreno's *Sociometry*, and the Tavistock Institute. Key individuals associated with INSNA have included Linton C. Freeman and Barry Wellman.

Along the way, INSNA developed the concepts and technology for what are now known as "social media."

Facebook's Mark Zuckerberg and other profiteers of the police state were simply graduate students of some of the initial leaders at INSNA. At the height of the East German police state, a former colonel suggested that about one person in eight was an informer; with Facebook and other social media, nearly everyone is an informer.

III. Genius as the Enemy

There is one final, overarching issue to settle concerning the oligarchy's top-down manipulation using the methods described here. It is not merely a matter of large-scale manipulation of the population, nor the use of such methods to overthrow legitimate governments and push the world closer to war. There is also the paramount concern of the British Empire, as emphasized by Bertrand Russell, that "after pupils have left school, they shall be incapable, throughout the rest of their lives, of thinking or acting otherwise than as their schoolmasters would have wished."

Bluntly stated, the enemy for Russell is creative individual human thought.

Again, from that standpoint, it not surprising to see a convergence of psychologists and mathematicians on the field of social networking theory. The Tavistock Institute, *Sociometry*, and related institutions such as the Frankfurt School, have devoted great effort to the eradication of individual human genius. In social networking analysis, individuals are classified according to their animal appetites. And sub-networks are created to service different offshoots from the main branches. Statistical studies are performed to predict—and ultimately to manipulate—how groups of people will respond to certain stimuli or possible changes. It is all herd dynamics, dressed up in fancy language.

Early on, those who don't fit the pattern, those with a penchant for independent thought, those who have the courage to fight back, are identified. They are targeted to be culled from the herd—not necessarily killed, unless they rise to the threat level of a Martin Luther King or a Lyndon LaRouche, but minimally to be ostracized and "broken."

Such targeting is more pervasive than you might think. With personal histories gleaned from Facebook and other sources, the means to carry it out are now very sophisticated. During the hey-day of the FBI terror, in the 1940s and 1950s, many key individuals of courage and creativity were attacked in this manner, including Albert Einstein, Paul Robeson, and Wilhelm Furtwä„ngler. The methods employed by the FBI were effective, but they were incredibly crude compared to what is available today to isolate and destroy the enemies of Empire.

Gordon Allport was one of Tavistock's top operatives in the United States.

As Lyndon LaRouche has repeatedly insisted, it is human creativity—real individual moral genius—that changes history, that is responsible for all that has been positive in the development of the human species. It is the intent of the British Empire and its shallow puppets like Barack Obama to snuff it out, to enforce conformity and mediocrity everywhere. In the field of social network analysis, where every mouse click, every blog post, every "friend" is analyzed by mathematicians, sociologists, and psychologists, such creative individuals are identified as "cognitive generators"—potential leaders who develop original thought and inspire others. These are individuals who, at a key "nodal point," might disrupt and ruin the functioning of the social network, who might lead it in an undesired direction.

The social control witch-doctors for the oligarchy are right to worry. We have witnessed their inability—except for escalating further toward war—to deal with Vladimir Putin. And they are certainly incapable of dealing with the creative force that Lyndon LaRouche has unleashed through his Manhattan Project. The approach of the Manhattan Project is to *speak the truth* to falsehood and inspire citizens through *beauty*—the one method against which today's descendants of Bertrand Russell are helpless.

II. Why Americans Don't Respond to Reality

ZEPP-LAROUCHE IN SAN FRANCISCO

The Choice Before the United States

This is an edited transcript of Helga Zepp-LaRouche's keynote address to the Schiller Institute's June 8 Strategic Seminar in San Francisco, which drew 70 guests and experts to discuss, "Will the United States Join the New Silk Road? Global Scientific Development or Nuclear War."

If you look at the world situation—especially you the American public, who know almost nothing about it—people in Europe know a little bit more—but if you compare the immediate danger of an escalation of a confrontation between NATO, the United States, and Great Britain on the one hand, and Russia and China on the other,— public knowledge about it is so little that for me, this is actually the more scary aspect. Because the absence of public debate on the possible extinction of all civilization may be because of the indifference of many people, because they just don't care; or it may be that they are too scared to think it through. But the lack of a public debate is what we have to change.

So therefore, what I am going to say is not only meant to be food for thought—and I really want you to think about it—but it is also meant to be food for action. Start with the first immediate situation, which is the war danger.

For about two days, maneuvers have been underway in the Baltic states and Poland, where there is a remarkable combination of four NATO exercises. The most prominent is Anaconda 2016. It includes 30,000 soldiers from 24 nations, including 14,000 Americans and 12,000 Poles; 1,130 parachute drops; the crossing of the Vistula River; a night-time assault; 35 helicopters; and 3,000 vehicles, along with naval vessels.

Together with the other three exercises in the Baltic states, there are more than 60,000 troops in maneuvers right now on the border of Russia. I can tell you that it is the first time since Hitler and his Operation Barbarossa that that number of troops has massed at what was then the Soviet border; it's the first time since the beginning of the 1940s that this has occurred.

Obviously, when you have this many troops in exercises—rehearsing the non-existent threat of Russia attacking the Baltic states—then there is a danger that an accident could happen. You could have an escalation. The warning time is a couple of minutes, so you could have a rapid deterioration of this situation into a large war. The *Guardian*—this is a British newspaper—quoted an unnamed European defense attaché saying this is a nightmare scenario, because a mishap could lead to a great danger. I wouldn't call it a matter of a mishap. I say it is the largest provocation, intended to compel Russia to capitulate. But will it capitulate? Obviously not.

Just a couple of weeks ago in Romania, the U.S./NATO anti-ballistic missile (ABM) system was completed and went live—the ABM system that many Russian experts have said is intended to destroy the capability of the Russian nuclear arsenal. Two years ago at a conference in Moscow, video animations were used to demonstrate that the entire ABM system which Obama has been steadily building, has only one aim, and that is to prepare for a first strike on Russia, by taking out its second-strike capability. Russia said, of course, that it cannot—it will not—accept that this ABM system be built beyond a certain point, because when Russia becomes indefensible, obviously, then it will be too late.

The Forgotten Lesson

The whole ballistic missile defense system supposedly was directed against Iranian missiles. Everyone knew from the beginning that that was a lie. Russia repeatedly offered to have such installations in the South of Russia, much closer to Iran, which the United States refused. And now, since the signing of the P5+1 agreement with Iran, such a threat no longer exists. Furthermore, Putin has proposed to Obama many times that the threat which Russia sees in this ABM system be dis-

Soldiers with the U.S. Army's 173rd Airborne Brigade jump off a Polish helicopter during NATO's Anakonda exercise in Poland, June 10, 2016. The exercises in Poland involve 31,000 participants.

which was the idea that no one side can use nuclear weapons, because it will lead to the annihilation of everybody; but that idea of Mutually Assured Destruction has been replaced by a utopian conception, that with modern technology and smarter weapons you can actually win a nuclear war.

President Obama, when he took office, promised he would work toward a nuclear-free world. He got the Nobel Peace Prize for that. If you look at it, he has just recently committed the United States to spend a trillion dollars to modernize all of its nuclear arsenals, including tactical nuclear weapons installed mostly in Europe, the so-called B61-12 bombs, which are supposed to be put on stealth bombers, and then sneak through the air defense of the opponent, meaning Russia, and disarm it in a first strike. They are supposed to be "more usable" that current bombs. Now recently in hearings in the U.S. Senate, Senator Dianne Feinstein commented on that, and said the very idea of having new, modernized nuclear weapons which are supposedly "more usable," is already an utterly immoral idea.

Right now, we're a the situation where beginning of July in the NATO summit in Warsaw, they intend to emplace battalions at the Russian border in the Baltics, they want to beef up the equipment, move heavy armament into Poland, into the Baltic States, and arm the Ukrainian forces deployed against the Eastern Ukraine. They want to link up the Romanian ballistic missile system with the Aegis destroyer warships in the Baltics, in the Black Sea. And all of this has reached a point of utmost provocation.

But one should be very clear, and that has also been expressed by many military experts, with all of this big moving of troops into Poland, into Estonia, Lithuania, what does it all amount to? Nothing! Because if it came to war, these conventional forces would be overrun by the Russian army in no time. And there is general agreement among military experts that they therefore only constitute a so-called "tripwire" condition, mainly

cussed. And Obama has flatly refused to even discuss it. So there are now arguments appearing that correctly make the point that there is only one explanation for the refusal to discuss it, and that is indeed, that the United States is preparing a surprise attack on Russia.

Normally you would say this is crazy, this cannot be, because if you use nuclear weapons,— People have forgotten the stark lessons from the Cuban Missile Crisis, and that President Kennedy said at that time, if it comes to nuclear war, those who die in the first hours will be happy as compared to those who die a couple of weeks later, or who die as a consequence of the nuclear winter, because those will die a much more miserable death. That lesson has been forgotten. It has been ignored.

But the NATO doctrine has been changed for the worse since the time of the Cuban Missile Crisis, and since the strategic confrontation of the medium-range missile crisis in the 1980s, when the SS-20 and the Pershing 2 were directed against each other with only a few minutes' warning time. At that time there were hundreds of thousands of people in the streets in Europe, warning that if it comes to nuclear war, then it would be the end of human civilization.

Today, experts assess the danger of nuclear war as far greater, for a number of reasons. One reason is the junking of the Mutually Assured Destruction doctrine, being the pretext, where some kind of an incident then creates the precondition for war.

Danger in the Pacific

Now if it comes to war,— and that has been stressed just today in a comment by the Russian Ambassador in Denmark, where somebody said to him, obviously Russia makes a fierce response to these maneuvers, and the Russian Ambassador to Denmark said, "No, we will not dramatize these maneuvers. We'll just keep a very sharp eye. And people should just be aware that if it comes to war, it will be a general war, which nobody can want." Now Russia is obviously reacting to it. They're taking their own military measures. They're putting more troops into the various bases in the Northern Military District. They are making their own maneuvers against the intrusion of Aegis destroyer ships in the Black Sea, pilots training to take out these Aegis ships, which are part of the system. But this all shows you how extremely dangerous this is. And we are sitting on top of immediate war danger right now; and the people in the United States do not even know about it.

Now unfortunately, this is not the only spot of potential war danger. The other one is related to China, because the confrontation against China is exactly of the same nature as that against Russia. One of which is the South China Sea. Now when you listen to the western media, you will hear about the alleged aggressive land grabbing of China in some of these islands in the China Sea, most of which are just rocks. But in reality, it is nothing of that sort.

If you look at the map, the South China Sea islands are all in the relative vicinity of China, and since the 9th Century have been regarded as Chinese territory. China has expressed that by the so-called Nine Dash Line, showing what its claims are. And in the recent period the United States started to make the point that China is fortifying some of these islands, building landing strips, which China is doing. But so have all the other countries done,— Vietnam, the Philippines, have all done the same thing. And Washington is clearly moving to create a similar provocation.

Now the Philippine government, still under the old government, went to the Hague, to the International Arbitration Court, and said that these claims are not le-

gitimate; and basically, it's expected that the Hague Court, soon in September will come out with a ruling against China. People have to understand that there are laws and agreements; for example, there is the United Nations Convention on the Law of the Sea, the so-called UNCLOS. And for the parties in the South China Sea, the DOC, which has been signed by all the countries from this region, which says that nobody would unilaterally seek arbitration, but that every territorial controversy would be negotiated on the bilateral level through negotiation and diplomacy. And therefore, China has taken the position that the effort to take this to an International Court, which is not recognized by China, is actually a violation of International Law.

There have been deliberate violations of the 12-mile zone by U.S. warships or overflights of these islands by U.S. fighter jets; and it is very clear that at a certain moment, China may assert its right to put up an air defense system, an ADIZ system. And at that point we are probably looking at a showdown, at the potential that it gets out of control.

Okay, now let's take a step back. What is this all about? Why are we staging military provocations at several spots in the world,— at the Russian border in Eastern Europe, at the South China Sea, and around South and North Korea with the threat of the United States to station THAAD missiles, missiles which look very far into the territory of Russia and China, and are not just aimed against North Korea? Then naturally the

mda.mil

A Terminal High Altitude Area Defense (THAAD) ballistic missile interceptor is launched during a Nov. 1, 2015 test.

whole situation in Southwest Asia, which is still a complete powder keg; despite the fact that the situation in Syria has been stabilized by President Putin's intervention. Why are we at the verge of World War III? What is the cause? What is the issue?

The Unipolar Illusion

Well, it all comes back to when the Soviet Union disintegrated in 1991. As recent decisions make clear without question of doubt, there were promises given to Gorbachov, to Chancellor Kohl, to Genscher, and to others, that if Germany were allowed to unify, and be part of NATO, then NATO would absolutely not expand to the borders of Russia. Now recent archived materials have documented the truth of what was said by the former U.S. Ambassador Matlock and others, that these promises were given, and that was part of how the Cold War ended.

But at the same time, Secretary of State Baker had already made moves to do exactly the opposite: namely to move NATO troops closer to the border, and to win over more members of the former Warsaw Pact to join NATO. And as Victoria Nuland has publicly stated, the State Department spent just in the case of Ukraine, $5 billion for regime change, for color revolution. And all of this was an attempt to encircle Russia, with the idea of finally causing regime change in Russia; and by the same logic also in China.

Now the logic behind that is, that at the moment when the Soviet Union disintegrated, there was a unique chance to have a peace order for the 21st Century, because the enemy was gone; Communism had disintegrated. And why not establish a peace order, which would have created a basis for the ending of war; and for finally attending to those issues which are in the common interest of all of mankind? Now we of the La-Rouche Movement and the Schiller Institute, we proposed exactly that. We proposed first, the Eurasian Land-Bridge, the New Silk Road, and we kept pushing the idea of uniting Europe and Asia through development corridors, as the basis for a peace order, and we always invited the United States to be part of that.

Unfortunately, you had at that time the neo-cons in the United States. Already in 1997 the neo-cons had developed the idea of a Project for a New American Century, which was the idea that, okay, the Soviet Union is the enemy, and now is the time to have a unipolar world, and to go for regime change against anybody who doesn't submit to this order. The idea that the United States, together with Great Britain—based on the "Special Relationship" with the British—would have an empire; and would not allow any one nation or a group of nations to ever become economically, politically, or militarily as strong as the United States, to bypass the United States. And therefore regime change, color revolution, or military intervention as we have seen it in Iraq, Syria, Libya, Afghanistan, would be legitimate.

Obviously this is an illusion, because the unipolar world has long ceased to exist. Asia is rising, bypassing the United States. They are already exporting more high-technology goods; they are already producing more high-technology scientists and engineers than the United States. China's economic growth rate —even when it went down from 12% in the coastal areas, 10% generally, to *only* about 7%—is still significant growth. India is even bigger; they have 8%. China and India together have 2.5 billion people. One of every three humans is Indian or Chinese.

Since China launched the New Silk Road initiative, 70 countries have joined in this kind of economic cooperation; and it's expected that by the end of year, it will be 100 nations, working in win-win cooperation with China, with Russia, and with India. And therefore, the idea of maintaining a unipolar world by military domination, by drawing people into military alliances for confrontation against Russia and China, is simply a no-win perspective.

That was just very, very clear a the recent Shangri-La Security Summit in Singapore, where U.S. Defense Secretary Ash Carter tried to impose a NATO-like structure for Asia. It did not go over so well, because Japan is now moving more with Russia, and the Vietnamese invited the Chinese for military maneuvers. So it didn't go over so well, because many countries realize that they have the choice right now between either joining World War III on the side of the United States, or to keep going into a cooperation with the BRICS countries, with the Asia-centered Silk Road. Therefore, the idea that it's possible to maintain a unipolar world simply will not succeed.

Now however, how do we get out of this? How do we get the United States to recognize that it's not in their best interest to do this? Because, eventually, if it comes to a global war, it will lead to the destruction of all of mankind. Given the present combination of governments from the Bush administration to Obama, I don't think that an appeal to pure reason is going to work.

Therefore, I want to focus on the significance of the

28 pages. Most of you are aware of the subject. For those of you who are watching and listening, let me just very briefly summarize it, again. The 9/11 attacks occurred. Then there was a Congressional investigation of both Houses, the Congress and the Senate, headed by Sen. Bob Graham. They published an official report; and of this report, 28 pages were classified. President Obama, in his election campaign, had promised the families of the 3,000 victims of the attacks that he would publish those pages, because these people have the right to know why their relatives died.

September 11

In the meantime, a whole movement has been created for the release of these 28 pages. Some Congressmen have read them; they were allowed to read them but not talk about them, because they were still classified. A lot of information has come out in various forms since, which makes very, very clear that what these 28 pages signify, is the role of Saudi Arabia in the financing of the September 11 attacks. The question then becomes, who in the United States was complicit in the cover-up? Everything points to the role of the FBI, among others.

Recently, the Senate passed the so-called JASTA bill (Justice Against Sponsors of Terrorism Act), allowing civil suits against Saudi Arabia to go ahead in this context. Why is this so important? Just take it a step back. What did September 11 do? It not only changed the Constitution in the United States. It eliminated many, many civil liberties. It allowed the limitless surveillance of not only American citizens, but citizens around the world, through the National Security Agency (NSA). In terms of foreign policy, it not only gave the go ahead for the war against Afghanistan; it was also the pretext for the war against Saddam Hussein. Remember the famous so-called "weapons of mass destruction," which never existed. The war against Qaddafi, the attempt to topple Assad, the *total* destruction of the Middle East and Northern Africa.

And naturally, that has to be stated very clearly: Europe right now is *completely destabilized,*— to the point of the detonation of the European Union,— through an unprecedented refugee crisis. Or, rather, the last time there was something like that was at the end of World War II, when millions of people marched across Europe and Asia as a consequence of the Second World War. Now you have millions on the march, from the Middle East, from Northern Africa, trying to get into Europe; and Europe is falling apart as a consequence. And nobody dares to talk about the so-called "root causes" of this refugee crisis. But the root causes are wars based on lies, based on the lies of September 11.

So therefore, if this document were published—and now the demand is not only to publish that, but also the 80,000 pages withheld by the FBI which were never given to the September 11 Commission—then, naturally, the whole policy would have to be reviewed and rejected. The role of Saudi Arabia in financing ISIS and al-Nusra, the continuous supply of ISIS by Turkey; all of this would come out. And maybe it would cause a big upheaval; but that upheaval is absolutely necessary to stop this present drive into World War III.

I appeal to you that one of the very clear leverages you American citizens have to intervene, is the publication of these 28 pages, which by no means are just a single issue—the question of who did September 11. But given the fact that already in the German media, there was a prime-time TV program called *Monitor* on June 1 said that when the 28 pages come out, the entire history of 9/11 will have to be rewritten,— getting to one of the keys to the strategic situation, one second before 12:00 midnight,— I hope.

Let me introduce the third subject I want to talk about. The solution to all of this would be a piece of cake. It is already there! A New Silk Road has been launched. We called it in 1989, first, the Productive Triangle; in 1991 we called it the Eurasian Land-Bridge. The New Silk Road was the idea that when the Iron Curtain had fallen, we would integrate the populations of the industrial centers of Europe with those of Asia, through development corridors. This New Silk Road program would have changed the world in the direction of a peace order, already in 1991; but, unfortunately, you had Bush, Sr., you had Margaret Thatcher, you had François Mitterrand, who all had completely different ideas. They wanted to reduce Russia from a superpower to a Third World, raw-materials-producing country, and they imposed the "shock therapy" of the Yeltsin period. They dismantled the Russian potential, and said they had no intention of allowing Germany to have any kind of economic relation with Russia. So it did not happen.

You had the 1990s, the time of genocide against Russia. You had all of the consequences of the Bush period. You had the eight years of Clinton, which were a certain interruption; but then with Bush, Jr. and Obama, you went back to the old project of an American Century doctrine and the idea of a unilateral world.

China's Offer

Fortunately, in 2013, President Xi Jinping announced the New Silk Road to be *the* strategic objective of China. In the almost three years which have passed since, this idea of ending geopolitics, of establishing win-win cooperation among all nations on the planet in the tradition of the ancient Silk Road, is progressing extremely quickly. Remember, the ancient Silk Road was a fantastic cooperation in terms of exchange of culture, goods, paper, technology, porcelain, silk, silk-producing, and many other cultural manifestations. It led to a tremendous benefit for all the countries which participated, from Asia to Europe.

The New Silk Road, obviously, is doing exactly that. The amount of projects which have been concluded between China and ASEAN countries, China and Latin American countries, China and Europe, China and African countries, China and East European countries, and now, in a very clear fashion, the economic integration between the Eurasian Economic Union, headed by Russia, and the New Silk Road, is progressing very well. An alliance has been formed between Russia and China, with India being the third factor in the situation. Many, many other countries have been joining.

Contrary to what you read and hear in the mass media, China is not doing badly. They are shifting their economic orientation from an export orientation, because the export markets in the trans-Atlantic sector are shrinking. They are now going more into infrastructure investment in many countries of the world, and to developing the inner region of China. To raise the consumer to a higher standard in their own population, since they have lifted 600 million people out of poverty, into a decent living standard in China. This is indeed the absolutely correct policy, to say we will uplift the remaining people who are still poor, and also allow them to participate in the Chinese economic miracle.

Xi Jinping has offered to President Obama that the United States join. The United States should also rebuild Southwest Asia, which I think is the moral obligation of the United States, given the fact that they were the key reason why these countries are now in such disarray. It should also participate in the building of Africa, which I think the West has an absolute moral obligation to do: Because the reason why you have millions of people as refugees,— not only risking their lives drowning in the Mediterranean, but also dying in the Sahara,

Xinhua/Rao Aimin

So far, 70 countries have joined China's New Silk Road initiative. Here Chinese President Xi Jinping attends the 23rd APEC Economic Leaders' Meeting in Manila, the Philippines, Nov. 19, 2015.

which has even more victims than even the Mediterranean,— is because *50 years* of IMF policy has denied economic development to Africa!

And the reason that people are taking the risk of a 50% chance that they will die, to cross the Mediterranean, is because they are running from war, from hunger, from epidemics, and this is the result of Western policy denying this continent economic development!

So we have a moral obligation to join hands to develop southwest Asia, to develop Africa.

Now, the United States also needs a Silk Road. If you look at the figures of the U.S. Bureau of Labor Statistics, of the productivity, which has collapsed for seven years in a row, all the indices are going down. The United States population is in a *terrible* condition, or at least in the poorer parts, while the rich become richer and Wall Street is having a heyday with cocaine parties and plotting destruction for the rest of the world.

But the United States needs an infrastructure project: the roads are bad, the traffic is ridiculous. People spend hours and hours every day in commuting, taking the risk of disappearing with their cars into a pothole. They have no rail system: China has built a 20,000 km fast train system through the end of last year; they plan to have 50,000 km by the year 2020, uniting every major city in China through a fast train system. And these are fantastic—they're smooth, they're fast, they're quiet. How many kilometers of fast train systems has the United States built? Zero!

So, for the United States to build its own Silk Road, to connect with the global development perspective, is a question of the best action for self-interest. And we have to get the United States off this confrontation course, and simply say, we have to shift from this policy and all the trillion-dollar investment in modernization of nuclear arsenals and the largest military budget in the world, trying to maintain an empire which is collapsing anyway. Rather shift; get rid of Wall Street; impose Glass-Steagall; get back to a policy of Alexander Hamilton, a credit policy; invest in infrastructure and go in the direction of a win-win cooperation with the other nations of the world: With Russia, China, European nations, with India; build up Latin America, build up Africa and Southwest Asia.

What Is More Important?

So this is really the choice before the United States. And I know it is very difficult for you to grasp how this should be done, but, you know, think about Kennedy; think about the kind of optimistic country the United States used to be. Think about the idea that America was built to be "a beacon of hope and a temple of liberty," where people from the whole world would go and try to be free. The U.S. sings in the National Anthem, "the land of the free" — is the United States "the land of the free" today? I don't think anybody who is in their right mind would say that today.

So, go back to the values of the American Republic, as it was founded by people like Benjamin Franklin, or George Washington; go back to the policies of Alexander Hamilton, Franklin D. Roosevelt, Kennedy, Martin Luther King. And I think if the United States could mobilize itself to bring back that nation, the whole world would love to be friends of the United States again. Right now, I can tell you, the rest of the world has almost given up on the United States, and then they look at the election process, the choice between a very, very irrational Trump and unfortunately a very, very predictable Hillary Clinton, given her statements about confrontation against Russia and China,— I think you have to really mobilize now. And I think the 28 pages, Glass-Steagall, these are flanks which can derail the situation long before this election takes place.

So we have to have a completely new world. In a certain sense, remember, mankind is not a beast, and mankind is not bound to do what seems to be inevitable, but mankind is the only species capable of reason, ca-pable of free will, of defining and designing a beautiful future, and going to implement that which the last time with Kennedy, was the Apollo Project,— and I think we can absolutely do it again! I think you have a great possibility in front of you, and I would encourage you: Be American. Be true Americans again, and the whole world will be most happy and embrace you. [applause]

Question: Helga, my name is K— from Silicon Valley, and the question I have is how do we deal with the fear that I feel exists in our culture, about really having the courage to speak out about the kinds of things you're discussing? I think really down deep, I think all of us truly want peace in the world; and yet we feel that those of us who speak out, against, if you will, "the club" you mentioned earlier, we seem to get chastised and labeled as radicals. I happen to tend to be on the right side of the political world, and when I attend LaRouche events, I'm chastised by some of my colleagues who say, "What in the hell are you doing?" And how do we deal with that?

Zepp-LaRouche: I think it's the question of, can you look into the mirror in the morning—you know, what is more important? Is it more important to be accepted by your stupid neighbors, and your colleagues when they're thinking stupidly? Or is it more important that you are truthful, that you uphold principles which are the important principles of the Universe and of mankind?

I think it's very important that you make a distinction: Do you want to be a shallow-minded opportunist, going with public opinion just to be in the flow? Or do you want to be a truthful person? And I think the only people who are worth anything, are those people who are searching for the truth, no matter if it's science, culture, or political truth. And I always tell people, if you think through where we are at, it's okay to have fear. Fear is actually a good thing. If children didn't have fear,— and some children have to be taught what are the dangers, because they would jump out of a window, they would put their hand into the oven, they would take matches and burn down the house; because they don't yet have the sense of real danger.

So fear, *per se*, is not a bad thing. Fear is actually something which is part of the survival instinct. Without fear you cannot survive. But, fear has to be located in the right thing, and not an irrational fear. Fear of the stupid opinion of your neighbor is really *nothing* compared to the fear of the possibility of the annihilation of mankind in a nuclear war. Or, for that matter, in a financial system breaking down in chaos, because we are equally close to a collapse of the trans-Atlantic financial system, which if it happened, would lead to chaos, and out of the chaos would come, for sure, also war.

So if you think about what could happen with these maneuvers, with this confrontation policy toward Russia and China, you could have a situation where nuclear war happens: And what would that mean? Have you ever thought about what that would mean? It would mean that everything you did, your family, your ancestors, all the great minds of the past, of Abraham Lincoln, of Beethoven, of Einstein, all of this would have been for nothing! Because there would be absolutely nobody to even remember that they existed. There would be no museum to keep the record, it would all vanish.

Now, for me, that is a real fear, because I think that mankind has produced so many beautiful things, like the great Classical compositions, or the great dramas, all the many beautiful cultures which have developed around the world; I think that that is the fear you should have, really. And in a certain sense, you must become free, your *inner self* has to become free. And Friedrich Schiller developed this conception in two very beautiful writings of his, which are called, *On the Sublime*. And there, he describes this and says, when man is only a physical beast, a physical creature, then fear can take over very easily, because even a bear is stronger, a tiger can eat a man, and therefore, as long as you are only a physical person, fear dominates you. But man is not just that: Man has the ability to connect his or her identity to universal principles which are more immortal than your physical existence, and of a higher value than you as a person.

Now, Schiller says, if you do that, and you locate your identity in the universal history of all of mankind, or other great principles, then you may not be physically safe because a lion can still eat you for breakfast, but your inner person is free. You are morally free. And then you are not afraid of things which you should not be afraid of. And I think the whole struggle of all us, is to continuously work on this idea of inner freedom, because if you don't think, if you can be intimidated, then you are nothing but a slave. And I think that that is a condition which we should all absolutely abhor, and reject as not being in cohesion with human dignity.

So be courageous and develop your inner freedom, and then you will be funny and laugh at your stupid neighbors, and be ironic, make polemics, and then, very, very soon, they will realize you are the wise man, and they are the children who have to learn from you.

How 'Geopolitics' Is Isolating America

by William Jones

June 12—U.S. Defense Secretary Ashton Carter's "show of force" at this year's Shangri-La Dialogue of defense ministers from around the world, in Singapore June 3-5, was a non-stellar performance. He upbraided China for its actions in the South China Sea, where China is building lighthouses and other useful facilities, claiming that by such actions, China was "isolating itself," and "jeopardizing" its participation in that "principled security network" which the United States is intent on building in the Asia-Pacific region.

It is something of an idle threat, as that "network" is based on the traditional Cold War alliances of the United States in the region, and is targeting China and Russia. It is somewhat like Br'er Fox inviting Br'er Rabbit into his lair. But the conflict in the region is by no means a kind of "Thucydides trap" between a rising power and a hegemonic power, as is being widely touted. It is, rather, a conflict between the choice of two different directions that mankind may take as it moves forward in the 21st Century.

Looking back over the last two decades, we can detect two clearly distinct roads traveled. We have in Europe and in the United States, in particular, the unfolding of the worst financial crisis in centuries. The London-New York financial system—which virtually hijacked the Rooseveltian vision for the Bretton Woods System right after Roosevelt's death in 1945—is in a state of advanced collapse. People are just waiting for the next shoe to drop.

In Asia, however, there is clear motion toward economic development, propelled primarily by China's success in bringing 600 million people out of poverty within two decades, an achievement previously unknown in world history. The newly-minted Belt and Road project of Chinese President Xi Jinping and the development of new financial structures associated with it—aimed solely at promoting infrastructural investment in the developing as well as the developed world—have created a great wave of optimism among the mass of mankind, especially those living below the equator, who hitherto have had little to say in giving direction to the world. While China has its own economic problems—contingent on the fact that its development has integrated it more closely into the faltering London-New York system—China is intent, to a large extent, on revamping that system in such a way that it can provide prosperity for the vast numbers of humankind.

Nations Kow-tow to U.S. but Join with China

Secretary Carter was really in la-la land when he claimed that the growth in Asia was the result of the military presence of the United States in the region since the end of the Second World War. Growth in the Asia-Pa-

DoD photo by Navy Petty Officer 1st Class Tim D. Godbee

Here, Defense Secretary Ash Carter (left) prepares to address the 15th International Institute for Strategic Studies Asia Security Summit in Singapore, June 4, 2016, as the Obama Administration attempts to encircle and contain China.

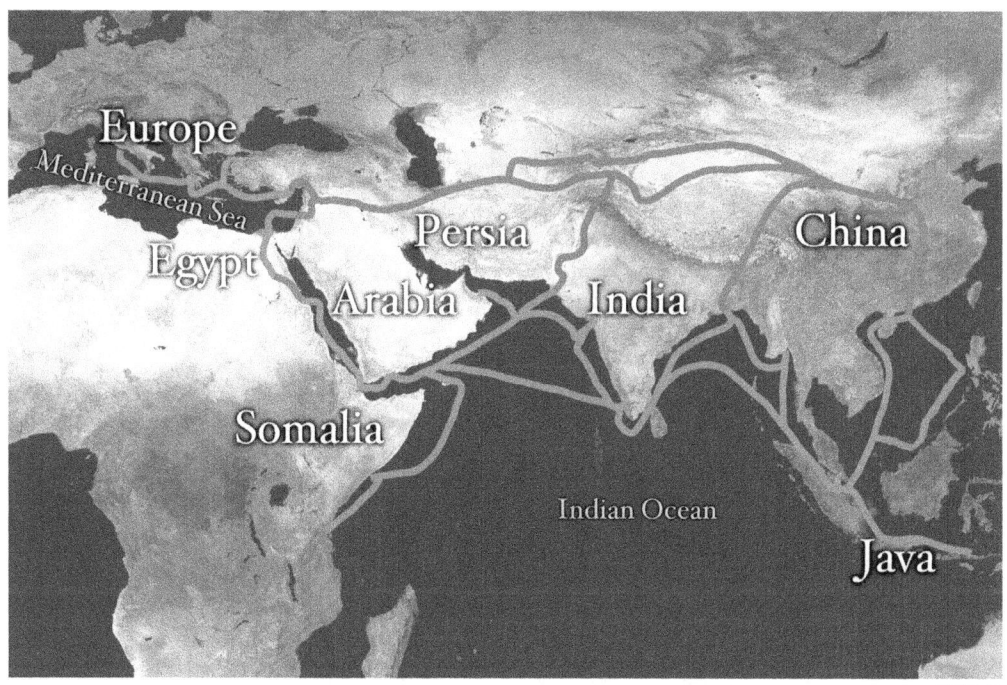
Wikipedia

China seeks a new basis for international relations with its Belt and Road initiative, based on building infrastructure projects globally.

cific region during the last three decades, while the United States has been totally focused on launching new wars in the Middle East, has been unprecedented, thanks to China's efforts to lift the 600 million people out of poverty, becoming the world's second major industrial producer in the process. The growth of China has fueled the growth of the entire region, and the initiation of the Silk Road Economic Belt and the 21st Century Maritime Silk Road by President Xi Jinping is intended to make regional development a permanent feature.

While Europe and the United States are still suffering the deleterious effects of trying to sustain the unpayable debt bubble, China, in collaboration with India, Russia, and other countries, is attempting to chart a new direction with the establishment of the Asian Infrastructure Investment Bank (AIIB) and the BRICS New Development Bank. And the majority of the countries of the world, which have been the greatest victims of the financial crisis, are experiencing a new wave of optimism about their future.

Until the launch of the Obama "pivot" to Asia—which has brought half of U.S. naval fire power to the Asia Pacific in an attempt to prevent China from asserting *any* of its legitimate territorial claims in the South China and East China seas—the Asia-Pacific region was doing quite well. Carter's latest gambit, his attempt

create a veritable NATO-like structure in the Pacific aimed at China and Russia, is only the latest stage in this outright policy of containment.

Carter exuded confidence that he had most of the Asia-Pacific countries on board this policy, and while many of the countries in the region may be somewhat nervous in the face of a country the size of China developing so rapidly, they have also understood the significance of that growth for their own development. They have joined almost without exception in the Chinese-initiated AIIB, and there is great interest in being part of the Belt and Road project for regional development. China's ambitious space exploration program has also created a tremendous amount of enthusiasm among a generation of leaders who have only a vague memory of the U.S. Apollo program. It is, of course, difficult for many countries to directly counter the United States when it demands cooperation, due to the U.S. ability to bully and coerce. Rather than show any affinity with U.S. intentions, which will ultimately result in nuclear war, they kow-tow to the United States on the ill-fated TPP while at the same time joining with China in a real development program.

Rooseveltian 'Community of Common Destiny'

President Xi Jinping has also called for the creation of a community of common destiny, harking back to what Franklin Roosevelt intended his United Nations to become. This idea also has a great appeal today as the developing nations of the world now feel the potential of their own power, as a formerly developing country, China, takes its place as a major world power. In his speech at Shangri-La, responding to Carter's bombast Admiral Sun Jianguo, Deputy Chief of China's Joint Staff, made a very incisive observation about U.S.

policy in the region and in the world: "We are not isolated today and we will not be isolated in the future," Sun said. "Actually, I'm worried that some people and countries [i.e., the United States] are still looking at China with a Cold War mentality and prejudice. They may build a wall in their minds and end up isolating themselves," he warned.

The cheap gimmick of another draconian "free trade" agreement like TPP pales into insignificance the light of what China is doing with the major infrastructure projects in connection with the Belt and Road Initiative. China's proposal is all-inclusive and aimed against no one, in contrast to Carter's NATO-like proposal, which targets China and Russia. Aware of the political and cultural diversity in the Asia-Pacific, China is setting down no fast and hard "rules of the road" that these countries must follow in working out their development strategies, but only considers the effects of the investment on the lives of the people concerned.

The recent perpetration of wars and random killings—by drone and otherwise—by the Bush and Obama Administrations has done much to tarnish the luster that the post-war United States had for many of these countries. And while countries may give some lip-service to U.S. demands, given the power of the United States to threaten and coerce, they know where their real interests lie—in preserving peace, harmony and development in the region, all of which would be mortally threatened by the outbreak of war.

Ironically, the direction of the New Silk Road Initiative may well revive in the Western nations those principles which allowed them previously to develop to their greatest potential. Western Europe is already getting a sense of this and is eagerly collaborating with China on the Belt and Road.

Return to an Industrial Policy

But this collaboration can only be successful if the nations reject the insanity of trying to prop up this unsustainable financial bubble known as the London-Wall Street system and return to the traditional notion of a government-directed industrial policy as a commitment of the nations to develop themselves.

If that were done, it would help reverse the obvious decline of the West. We could turn to rebuilding our na-

Xinhua

Chinese President Xi Jinping (left) announced his Belt and Road initiative while on a 2013 visit to Kazakstan. Kazakstan President Nursultan Nazarbayev (right) shown here during that visit.

tions, rebuilding livable cities, and developing more advanced technologies. We could fill the potholes, rebuild our roads, our highways, and our railroads. Our people could again view the future with hope, not despair. No doubt China would be willing to contribute to that effort, as it has already indicated in President Xi's repeated invitation to President Obama to join the project of building infrastructure for humanity.

Rather than preventing China from building high-speed rail networks here, we in the United States should be encouraging it, to help bring hope again to our continent. And we should drop the hopeless task of attempting to encircle China with a Great Wall of naval containment, a policy that can only lead to war. Let us encourage China to negotiate its territorial claims with its neighbors as China itself wishes to do. Or else, let us just stand aside and let the parties themselves resolve the issues.

Would it not be best to end this era of bloody "geopolitics," which has been so devastating for the United States and for the world, and to join with China, with Russia, with India, and with the rest of the world, in a project of economic development to make this world a suitable home for humanity, and to raise our sights to the firmament above to launch a program for expanding mankind's reach into the universe beyond, which is the ultimate home on which our existence depends?

Obama's Utopian War Madness

by Carl Osgood

June 12—Over recent months, there has been a growing chorus of warnings that the world is on the precipice of nuclear war, a war that will result in the end of human civilization. As part of that chorus, there has been an increasing exposure of the insane utopians whose theories dictate how nuclear weapons are to be used. The problem with these exposés, however, is that they assume that it is the utopians who are behind the danger, when it is in fact the collapse of the British imperial system of financier looting, a system of which President Obama is a willing asset, that is fueling the drive toward war.

As early as 1990, when the Berlin Wall had fallen and the Communist East Bloc was disintegrating, Lyndon LaRouche, from his jail cell in Rochester, Minnesota, was warning that it was not just the East Bloc that was collapsing, but that the West was also collapsing. The Soviet crisis, La-Rouche said in a Nov. 9, 1989 statement, was being accelerated by the collapse of the economy in the West, "especially the economies of the United Kingdom and of the United States, which contrary to all the talk about the boom in the United States, have been collapsing at varying rates, generally now accelerating since about 1970-71 with the events of that period."

LaRouche responded to the Soviet collapse with the "Paris-Berlin-Vienna Productive Triangle" policy, based on using that region, then still heavily industrialized, as a locomotive for world development. This was not, however, just an economic recovery policy, but also a war avoidance intervention.

"We are now at a point that, unless the railroad program, the Triangle Program, which we have specified for Central Europe, is implemented, we will have an international disaster," LaRouche said in February of 1990.

EIR video grab

In a 1999 video, LaRouche warned that British Empire-directed mercenaries, posing as Islamic, would ignite conflicts that would prevent collaboration of the Strategic Triangle nations, and ultimately lead to nuclear war.

"We might even have a new world war, erupting in the next couple of years, as a result of a failure to implement the Railroad Triangle program." Instead of heeding La-Rouche's warning, the George H.W. Bush Administration and the successive Tory governments in the Britain of Margaret Thatcher and John Major chose a different path, one of economic looting of the former Soviet bloc and expanding wars in the Balkans and the Middle East.

In 1999, LaRouche forecast where we would soon be if that policy direction were not changed—in fact, where we are now—in his *Storm Over Asia* video. The threat LaRouche identified was that of generalized global war not only against Russia, but also against Iran, China, and India.

"If these nations are pushed to the wall by a continuing escalation of a war which is modeled on the wars which the British ran against Russia, China, and so

Russian President Vladimir Putin (left) and China President Xi Jinping at Russian-Chinese talks on Sept. 3, 2015 in Beijing.

forth, during the Nineteenth Century and early Twentieth Century, this will lead to the point that Russia has to make the decision to accept the disintegration of Russia as a nation, or to resort to the means it has, to exact terrible penalties on those who are attacking it, going closer and closer to the source, the forces behind the mercenaries—which include, of course, Turkey, which is a prime NATO asset being used as a cover for much of this mercenary operation [that is, the terrorist wars that were then being run against Russia] in the North Caucasus and in Central Asia," LaRouche said.

Russia chose not to disintegrate, and under the leadership of President Vladimir Putin, has built up its capacity to resist. China has, in a similar fashion, built up its economy together with Russia and other nations, and is now offering the world its Silk Road policy—in effect, LaRouche's Land Bridge policy, first articulated in the mid-1990s—as humanity's alternative to economic collapse and nuclear war. The Anglo-American Empire, desperate to save itself from near-term extinction, has nothing left to offer except its insane utopian nuclear war strategy.

Insanity of 'Escalate to De-Escalate'

In 1983, neocon agents in the Reagan Administration ran a war game called "Proud Prophet," which was "a large scale, interactive, politico-military game which involved more than 200 people for 12 days of actual game play stretched out over seven weeks," according to the highly redacted, after-action report produced by the National Defense University in early 1984. What made the game unusual was that it involved actual decision-makers, including Secretary of Defense Caspar Weinberger and the Chairman of the Joint Chiefs of Staff, Gen. John Vessey. The roughly 200 participants were from a laundry list of U.S. government agencies and U.S. military commands around the world.

According to author and Defense Department advisor Paul Bracken, who has apparently written the most authoritative account of Proud Prophet so far, the war game involved actual U.S. war plans, making it "the most realistic exercise involving nuclear weapons ever played by the U.S. government during the Cold War."

The result? "Many of the strategic concepts proposed to deal with the Soviet Union were revealed to be either irresponsible or totally incompatible with current U.S. capabilities and immediately thrown out," Bracken writes. One of those concepts was the idea of de-escalatory nuclear strikes, the idea being that if the Soviets saw that NATO would go nuclear early, then they would back down and "come to their senses." But that is not what happened in the game.

"The Soviet Union team interpreted the nuclear strikes as an attack on their nation, their way of life, and their honor," Bracken writes. "So they responded with an enormous nuclear salvo at the United States." The United States retaliated in kind, and pretty soon there was nothing left of the world. "This game went nuclear big time, not because Secretary Weinberger and the chairman of the Joint Chiefs were crazy, but because they faithfully implemented the prevailing U.S. strategy," Bracken reports. The results of the game must have been particularly scary for President Ronald Reagan. "A nuclear war cannot be won and must never be fought," Reagan said in a subsequent State of the Union address.

Geoff Wilson and Will Saetren, both of the Ploughshares Fund anti-nuclear advocacy group, in a May 27 article in *The National Interest*, use the Bracken account of Proud Prophet to warn that the concept of nuclear de-escalation is today part of NATO planning, but it is just as insane now as it was then. The implication of Wilson and Saetren's argument is that Russia, today, would likely react the same way, resulting in a nuclear escalation that ends with massive nuclear exchanges, resulting in the end of the world. "The notion that nuclear weapons can be used for anything 'beyond deterrence' is reckless and dangerous thinking. It is an option that should be taken off the table entirely," they conclude.

This is the warning, in fact, that was issued by former Vice Chairman of the Joint Chiefs of Staff Gen. James Cartwright and retired Russian General Valdimir Dvorkin in an op-ed in the *New York Times* in April 2015. They also warned of the continued risk of a launch-on-warning operational posture. Cartwright's activities mark the revival of a long-standing fight between insane utopians, and sane military commanders engaged in active war avoidance today.

Irrationality of the SIOP

Numerous changes were made to U.S. nuclear strategy following Proud Prophet, but an underlying irrationality must have remained. In early 1991, Gen. George Lee Butler, who had just taken command of the U.S. Air Force's Strategic Air Command, asked to see the SIOP, the Single Integrated Operational Plan—the plan for waging global thermonuclear war against the Soviet Union. Author Eric Schlosser, in his book *Command and Control*, reports that Butler examined every single target in the SIOP, scrutinizing thousands of ground-zeros. What he found—and he was hardly naive, having spent much of his career in the nuclear business—astonished him. Bridges and rail-

Stevens Institute of Technology/youtube

The Proud Prophet war game in 1983, which used actual U.S. war plans, demonstrated that most of the U.S. nuclear war fighting concepts were wrong, according to a report by Paul Bracken (above).

USAF

After General George Lee Butler (above) took command of the U.S. Air Force's Strategic Command in 1991, he characterized U.S. nuclear war plans as "absurd and irresponsible."

roads in the middle of nowhere were targeted with dozens of warheads. Moscow itself was targeted with hundreds of warheads, including dozens of them aimed at a single radar station.

"With the possible exception of the Soviet nuclear war plan, this was the single most absurd and irresponsible document I had ever reviewed in my life," Butler later said, according to Schlosser. "I came to fully appreciate the truth … we escaped the Cold War without a nuclear holocaust by some combination of skill, luck, and divine intervention, and I suspect the latter in greatest proportion."

Butler traveled a road rare for such a high ranking military officer. He went from being responsible for waging a nuclear war to being an advocate for the abolition of nuclear weapons. Despite the rhetoric from President Obama about a world free of nuclear weapons, Butler is not much more sanguine about our chances today than he was in the 1990s. Nuclear war, of the kind he trained and planned for while in uniform, could still happen, Butler believes, because U.S. officials remain in the grip of the delusion that nuclear deterrence is an effective and safe policy.

In a May 27, 2016 profile published in *Politico*, Butler said that nuclear weapons policy making remains under the control of "a relatively small cadre of theorists and strategists who speak with great assurance and authority" but remain stuck "in the apocalyptic vocabulary of nuclear deterrence [and] worlds which spiral toward chaos." Deterrence, he says, is a "crutch that led to the expenditure of trillions of dollars" while "we ignored, discounted, or dismissed its flaws." He is particularly critical of the Obama Administration's policy of confrontation with Russia, which he believes has sacrificed opportunities for further reductions in nuclear weapons.

President Obama's stated commitment to denuclearization is completely fraudulent. Not only is he committed to the most expensive nuclear modernization program in U.S. history, but the rate of dismantling of nuclear warheads under his presidency has slowed to its lowest level since President John F. Kennedy. The Federation of American Scientists' Hans Kristensen reported in a May 26, 2016 blog posting—just as Obama was heading to Hiroshima, Japan—that the Obama Administration dismantled only 109 warheads in 2015, and that the administration dismantled the fewest warheads, as a proportion of the total stockpile, of any of the last three administrations.

The modernization program, in fact, includes weapons—the B61-12 nuclear gravity bomb and the Long Range Standoff cruise missile—that have been criticized as making nuclear weapons "more usable," in the words of General Cartwright. Both weapons are described as giving the president "more options" for their use, as opposed to large megatonnage strategic weapons that can only be used to destroy cities. "More options" means a greater temptation to use them—as in the case with the Euromissiles crisis of the 1980s—blurring the lines between conventional and nuclear war, all under "nuclear disarmament Nobel Peace Prize winning" President Obama.

Threat Inflation

Many top U.S. military officers have allowed themselves to be used to hype a non-existent Russian threat to the United States, as an "oh so clever" way to try to preserve their budgets.

The U.S. Army is feeling the budget pinch particularly hard, as it has shrunk from a post-9/11 high of 580,000 troops to 450,000, and may yet decline to 420,000. This shrinkage is occurring even as the Obama Administration is ramping up its confrontation and war threats against Russia.

These developments seem to be causing two contrary reactions in the Pentagon. One, not often reported, is to question the demonization of Russia in the first place,— while the other is to fly into panic mode and inflate the threat to persuade the U.S. Congress to jack up military spending. In a May 12 article in *Politico*, author Mark Perry recalled the April 5 testimony before the Senate Armed Services Committee of a panel of Army officers led by Lt. Gen. H.R. McMaster, the director of the U.S. Army Capabilities and Integration Center and widely regarded as one of the smartest men in the Army, in which the panel claimed that the Army is now in danger of being "outranged and outgunned" in the next war (which could only be against Russia and/or China) and that the Army is in danger of becoming "too small to secure the nation."

While the written testimony submitted by the panel seems to have been a consensus document among senior Army officers, not everybody, as Perry writes, was buying it. "This is the 'Chicken-Little, sky-is-falling' set in the Army," a senior Pentagon officer told him. "These guys want us to believe the Russians are ten feet tall. There's a simpler explanation: The Army is looking for a purpose, and a bigger chunk of the budget. And the best way to get that is to paint the Russians as being able to land in our rear and on both of our flanks at the same time [a reference to Gen. Grant's comment during the Battle of the Wilderness in 1864]. What a crock."

The reality is that the U.S. defense budget—when overseas contingency operations, the Department of Energy's portion of the nuclear weapons budget, and other ancillary war functions such as intelligence and homeland security are included—is close to $1 trillion a year. The Russian defense budget, in contrast, is a mere $84 billion. The numbers just don't add up the way those who are inflating the threat claim they do, to get a bigger budget.

Retired Army Colonel Douglas Macgregor, a fierce critic of the way the Army thinks, also blasted the McMaster testimony and those who say the Army needs a bigger budget to better protect the common soldier. "If the generals actually gave a damn about the soldiers, the last fifteen years would have been totally different," he wrote to Perry. "What happened to the thousands of lives and trillions of dollars squandered in Iraq and Afghanistan? What happened to the billions lost in a series of failed modernization programs since 1991?"

Indeed. If the generals who adapted to the geopolitical paradigm of perpetual warfare after 9/11, had instead told the truth as best they understood it, perhaps the series of disasters beginning with the attack on Afghanistan in October 2001, and the invasion of Iraq in March 2003 might have been avoided. That would have been the best defense of the United States they could have offered and a true adherence to their oaths as commissioned officers.

EDITORIAL

Hard Words; Who Can Hear Them?

June 9—Yesterday, probable FBI interference had almost succeeded in preventing Lyndon LaRouche's participation, via Internet, in a major Northern California conference organized by his associates. LaRouche would have been unable to participate but for a timely intervention by the leadership there.

Then, when LaRouche was finally able to speak, his starting point was the current acute threat to human existence.

> Well, the key thing I'm concerned about is the threats to the existence of the human species right now. Because at this time, the existence of the entire human species continues to be on the edge of jeopardy, and therefore we have to attune ourselves to understanding what the problems are that are involved in this, and what are the remedies for which we can get an escape for humanity in general.
>
> Humanity in general, right now, is under serious threat of jeopardy on a global scale. This does not mean that it has to happen that way. It means that if we do the right things, we can escape those threats, or at least have a reasonable ability to deal with those threats. That's where we stand, generally, right now. And if you want to do something about it, let's talk about it.

But from that moment forward, the whole tenor of LaRouche's remarks,— let's face it,— grated badly on the nerves of many listening. He kept coming back to the question of personal identity, but more especially of his own personal identity. To a question about how the individual mind overcomes obstacles to winning a battle for mankind, he answered:

> I can tell you, I'm still an active person, in society, and I'm a senior, and an experienced one, one of the most experienced of all people in that category. So I should think no one would have any difficulty in understanding who I am, what I am, where I came from and what I do.
>
> Somebody else may be clinging to an idea of a different identity of some other person, who I don't know, but it seems to be that.

LaRouche turned almost every question around in this way. This may be irritating to you, but the first question for you to ask is: Is it true? Do things "just happen," or are they "made to happen" by men and women who, as LaRouche said, are "qualified to make history"? When MacArthur was forced out of the Philippines on March 12, 1942, was he right to say, "I shall return," or should he have changed it to "We shall return?" Would mankind have made it to the Moon in 1969—or ever—but for the solitary figure of the first and greatest German space pioneer, Hermann Oberth (1894-1989)? Oberth spent most of his life in poverty. After fighting for his ideas of space travel for decades, he had met hardly anyone who both agreed, and understood their importance. But it is precisely to that "hardly anyone," like Wernher von Braun, that we owe the revolution which has been the space program.

To a question on how we can determine whether our

imagination is fantastic or truthful, LaRouche answered:

> Why don't we just say, let's identify a truthful example, a truthful personality, a truthful identity. *I am.* And anyone who would deny that, would be *mistaken*, misguided.
>
> I am known, I am identified, I am a figure of the history of most of the 20th Century, and most people from the 20th Century *should* know who I am, and they should know what I do. They may not know every detail of what I do, but that's it: I am a prominent and most prominent figure on this planet, among the most prominent ones.

Indeed, the later 20th Century would have been unrecognizable but for LaRouche's victory over the British system of economy in a Queens College, New York debate in 1971, which then led by circuitous routes to his victory for the Strategic Defense Initiative in the Reagan Administration by 1983. This in turn prepared the way for his initiative, with his wife Helga, which has now become the Eurasian Land-Bridge and the New Silk Road, which is the keystone development of the 21st Century to date.

Why is it so irritating to hear the obvious: that LaRouche is a key figure of the 20th and 21st Centuries? Because we were taught in school about the virtues of Democracy? Is that the real reason, or is it rather that we close our ears because we find it more comforting to us personally, to deny that any man or woman can actually be responsible for the human condition and the fate of humanity?

www.ingramcontent.com/pod-product-compliance
Lightning Source LLC
Chambersburg PA
CBHW081122280526
45787CB00007B/2945